DON'T PANIC :)

A LEGAL GUIDE
(IN PLAIN ENGLISH)

for

SMALL
BUSINESSES

and

CREATIVE
PROFESSIONALS

Version: June 2016

ISBN: 978-0-9976569-0-9

Book design and layout by Matthew Walker and Melissa Champaco

Illustrations by Batton Lash

Contents

Introduction

Welcome!

Ever wonder what sorts of issues you may encounter as a creator or entrepreneur, and when you might want to reach out to a real life lawyer? That's what this book is all about. This book is designed to help you through the legal issues you may run into as a creator, entrepreneur, or innovator.

We focus on issues you may encounter from the inception of your business to the moment (that hopefully doesn't happen) you get a nasty lawyer letter for the first time. While this book is not a substitute for legal advice, it can serve as a helpful guide to preventing and resolving legal issues.

Who is the ideal audience for this book?

Essentially, if you're doing something creative, launching a startup, or running a small business, this book is for you. If you or your business are any of the following, you're definitely in the right place:

- App & Software Developers

- Artists & Graphic Designers

- Bloggers & Journalists

- Clothing Designer

- Entrepreneurs, E-commerce Business People and Startups

- Filmmakers and YouTube creators

- Game Developers

- Makers

- Musicians

- Non-Profits

- Photographers

- Scholars & Researchers

- Writers and Publishers

Who are we and why should you listen to us?

We are New Media Rights. New Media Rights is a non-profit program that provides preventative, one-to-one legal services to creators, entrepreneurs, and internet users whose projects require specialized internet, intellectual property, privacy, media, and communications law expertise. You can read more about the types of services we provide, and see examples of the types of clients we work with, by visiting our New Media Rights Legal Services page[1]. This book is a culmination of 14 years of collective practical experience advising thousands of creators and entrepreneurs through the real life legal issues that they encounter. New Media Rights is an independently funded program of California Western School of Law, a 501(c)(3), and your purchase of this book supports our work to ensure all creators and innovators have access to legal services.

How to use this book

While we think there's quite a bit of value in reading the book cover to cover, the book is really designed so you can dip in to specific sections when you are encountering a particular issue or are at a particular stage of your work. In many sections we've also included a brief summary called "The Bottom Line," which gives you the essentials of that section in just a few sentences. It looks like this:

THE BOTTOM LINE

We've got tons of experience working with thousands of creators. Early legal guidance is often the difference between creative projects and businesses succeeding or dying on the vine. This book helps you understand what you don't know, which helps prevent legal issues before they start, and tells you when to go to a lawyer.

The only thing you should not do with this book is rely on it for legal advice. At the core of all good legal advice is a good lawyer who

---

1   "New Media Rights Legal Services." New Media Rights. 30 Oct. 2015.
     Web. <http://www.newmediarights.org/services_new_media_rights_offers>.

knows your specific situation. Although this book was written by a team of awesome lawyers and law students, we don't know the facts of your particular situation because we have not equipped this book with any creepy privacy-invading, mind-reading technology, and thus cannot give you legal advice. If you do need legal advice we strongly recommend talking to a qualified attorney to get the legal assistance you need.

One other caveat: the attorneys at New Media Rights are only licensed to practice law in California. Practically that means that this book will focus heavily on United States federal laws and California state law. If you've picked up this book outside of California or do business on a global scale, much of it will be useful, but there may be other state and international laws that apply to your situation and you should consult with a lawyer licensed to practice in those locations.

Questions & Comments

Have questions or comments about the book? Feel free to reach out to us via the New Media Rights contact form[2]. You can also find us on Twitter[3], Facebook[4] and YouTube[5].

2   "New Media Rights." Contact Us. New Media Rights, 1 Jan. 2016. Web. <http://www.newmediarights.org/about_us/contact_us>.
3   "New Media Rights Twitter." Twitter. New Media Rights. Web. <https://twitter.com/newmediarights>.
4   "New Media Rights Facebook." Facebook. New Media Rights. Web. <http://facebook.com/newmediarights>.
5   "New Media Rights YouTube." YouTube. New Media Rights. Web. <https://www.youtube.com/user/newmediarightsstudio>.

Part I
Getting Started

Chapter 1
Forming Your Business

So you're ready to take your project to the next level but don't know where to start. The first, and often the most important, step in making your project succeed is to formalize it as a business entity. Making sure your business is an actual legal entity can give you a higher level of credibility amongst professionals, investors, and consumers in your target market. There are also financial benefits like access to business loans, business bank accounts, and tax incentives, as well as legal benefits like limiting your personal liability.

The business model you select is arguably the most critical business decision you will make, so choose with caution. The choice requires plenty of research; an understanding of your business goals; and a lot of self-reflection. Will you need employees? Do you want full control of the business? How much time can you dedicate to the business? Will this be your only stream of income? These are just some of the questions you need to ask yourself before picking a business model. Since this is such an important decision and many of the business formation options below have very specific legal requirements, it is important to speak with a lawyer to make sure the business is formed correctly from the start. The following sections will give a general overview to help you understand some options for running your company whether you'd prefer to fly solo, work with a group, or even take a socially conscious approach.

I prefer to fly solo

Some people are very passionate about the vision, direction, and goals for their project. In some cases, it's easier to manage your creative vision alone. Although absolute control can be very stressful, it can be even more rewarding if it succeeds. Here are some business models that may be right for you if you prefer to fly solo.

1. **Sole Proprietor**

   If you start a business by yourself, the default business model is a Sole Proprietorship. This is a traditional business model where the owner is responsible for everything that happens in their business. As the name suggests, you will be in charge of everything including finances, day-to-day operations, and liability if anything goes wrong. The benefit of this model is that you get to control the direction of your business and can make changes immediately if needed. Another benefit is that you don't have to share the profits. But remember: "With great power comes great responsibility." As a Sole Proprietor you will be personally responsible for any legal disputes arising from your business. This model also requires a big investment of your time because you are responsible for everything in the business. Additionally, you have to keep clear accounting records because business taxes are filed under your personal taxes, which can make filing your taxes more challenging.

2. **Single Member LLC**

    Another option for someone looking to control their own business is establishing a Limited Liability Company. This option is very popular because it allows the owner to have the same level of control as a sole proprietor would, but with the limited liability of a corporation. What does that mean? Well if you follow your state's requirements in starting and maintaining your LLC, your personal assets will be protected from lawsuits against your business. This model requires several procedural formalities, like registering with the state, and many practical formalities, like keeping a separate bank account for the business. But if you don't maintain the LLC formalities and something happens, your personal assets could be on the line. Besides protecting your personal assets, choosing an LLC gives you the option to file taxes as a sole proprietor or as a separate corporation in addition to your own personal taxes. But you may be double taxed on the LLC's profits on your personal taxes.

I work well with others

Some people don't want to take on a project themselves and prefer a cooperative effort. Distributing responsibilities to others can give you more time to focus your efforts on the parts of the business where you have the most expertise. There are several options for a group of owners.

1. **Partnerships**

    A partnership is a good option if you started the project with other people that are equally as passionate about the project. Partnerships don't require many formalities, but most good partnerships use contracts to distribute responsibilities and profits. Partnership agreements are essential at the start of the business because they establish the ground rules for your partnership. The agreements should address things like basic operations, resolving partner disputes, and how to exit the partnership. Since partnerships require a group effort, it is important for everyone to be on the same page. Keep in mind partners will usually have equal control, equal profit, and equal liability, so make sure you trust the other partners before going down this path.

2. **Limited Partnership**

A limited partnership is great when some partners want to run the company while others stand back as investors. This model requires at least one general partner and one limited partner. The general partner has personal liability for the debts and obligations of the partnership. The tradeoff is that the general partner will have creative and operational control of the business, while the limited partner is not personally liable for any debt and obligation (as long as they are not involved in the operation of the business). If the limited partner does participate in the operations, they risk losing their "limited" status, and may then have personal liability as a general partner.

3. **Limited Liability Company**

The LLC model is very popular because it establishes the company as a separate entity under the law, which shields its members from personal liability and protects their personal assets. Liability protection is available whether the owner works hands-on as a member or a hands-off as an investor. This means that unlike a limited liability partnership a member will not lose liability protection if they are involved with day-to-day operations. However, to take advantage of this protection your state will require several strict procedural formalities like filing articles of organization, an operating agreement, and paying a minimum state tax. Another important requirement is that company assets and member assets are kept separate. Keeping assets separate will show that the company is treated as a separate entity and that owners never use business funds for personal use. An LLC usually pays the members individually through a salary, or profit sharing to keep assets separate. If these formalities are not met you can lose the limited liability protection, putting your personal assets on the line.

4. **Traditional Corporation**

A corporation is a great choice if the owners are more hands-off, and want to hire qualified people to run the company for them. Owners of a corporation have two layers of protection against liability. The first is that as shareholders, they appoint a board of directors to handle business decisions, which can shield shareholders from direct liability. The second layer involves the board hiring chief officers (CEO, CFO, COO etc.) to run the day-to-day operations, which separate shareholders further from liability. The protection from personal liability is the most attractive feature of a corporation because the shareholders can rest assured they will not be personally liable for the debts or actions of the corporation.

However, corporations are very formal and require strict procedures. The state will require minute-by-minute logs of board meetings to show the corporation is functioning as a separate entity. Additionally, be aware that corporations pay taxes on earnings, and shareholders pay taxes on their individual profits. Because corporations are so complex, and the requirements vary widely from state to state, you should work with an attorney to help you properly form your corporation.

It's not all about the Benjamins

Making money is a very important aspect of growing and maintaining a business. However, some business owners realize that contributing to society is equally important. Socially conscious business models range from giving percentages of profits to the community all the way to providing free services to folks who would otherwise go without. Here are some options for business formation to think about if your goals include making a positive impact on society through your business.

5. **Non-Profit Organization**

    A non-profit is an organization whose activities focus on public benefit and do not generate a private profit for individuals or shareholders. Going the non-profit route can be very satisfying because you can put making a positive impact on society above all other goals. If you obtain status as a 501(c)(3) exempt non-profit organization with the IRS, the big benefit is that the non-profit's donations and income related to its mission are generally not taxable. In return for this exemption from taxes however, non-profit organizations are strictly regulated. Remember that in order to receive non-profit tax-exempt status, the company needs to be incorporated as a non-profit under that state's laws and apply for federal and state tax-exemptions. If you're going the non-profit route, even as a small non-profit, you need to work with a lawyer, accountant, and others to make sure you're meeting all the accounting and administrative requirements. As far as control, you'll typically need to establish a board of directors for your non-profit, and it's the board that is ultimately entrusted with fulfilling the mission of the non-profit. This means you likely won't have as much control as you would have as an unincorporated entity. That said the strict requirements of running a non-profit may be worth it to be able to receive tax-free donations, and to be able to apply for various grants that are only available to non-profits.

6. Fiscal Sponsorship

This is a great model for early stage, small non-profit organizations. Before you create an entirely separate non-profit organization, consider working within a larger non-profit organization to incubate your organization. Once an established non-profit and the sponsored organization sign a fiscal sponsorship agreement, the sponsored organization is afforded tax-exempt benefits while working under the umbrella of that non-profit. A major benefit of fiscal sponsorship is the transfer of key administrative responsibilities to the larger non-profit. This transfer allows the sponsored organization to focus on their project instead of things like human resources and accounting. However, it is important to choose the right sponsor. Find an established non-profit that shares common goals with the sponsored organization, and that can handle the additional administration tasks. Also make sure to solidify any fiscal sponsorship arrangement in writing. If a non-profit is going to impose too many restrictions on your sponsored organization, you want to know that in writing up front. As with any contract, you should always consult an attorney to look over the sponsorship agreement. For more information on fiscal sponsorships check out our fiscal sponsorship guide.[6]

7. Benefit Corporations

Certain states have adopted this new class of business formation to allow corporations to bridge the gap between a for-profit corporation and a socially conscious non-profit organization. Traditional Corporations focus on maximizing profits, while Benefit Corporations allow executives to balance general public benefit with profit maximization.

6   Neill, Art, and Marko Radisavljevic. "Guide to Intellectual Property & Fiscal Sponsorship Agreements for Scientific, Research, and Archival Projects." New Media Rights, 03 Sept. 2014. Web. <http://newmediarights.org/guide_intellectual_property_fiscal_sponsorship_scientific_research_and_archival_projects>.

In California, Benefit Corporations must choose from a few specific benefits which include: providing low income communities with products or services, promoting economic opportunities for the community, preserving the environment, improving health, and promoting the arts and education. Due to the focus on public good, this model is attractive to socially conscious investors and consumers. Also, if executives make an unprofitable business decision to advance the corporation's social objective, they may be protected from liability. But unfortunately, the Benefit Corporation model is relatively new, and the lack of case law makes it hard to predict exactly how much protection would be afforded. In addition, there are no special tax breaks for choosing to operate as a benefit corporation.

1. B-Corp Certification

Not to be mistaken as a Benefit Corporation, a B-Corp is a certification, not a business formation. That being said, any type of corporate entity with a social goal can choose to become a certified B-Corp. To become certified, the company must complete and pass a specific assessment called an "Impact Assessment", which is normally done by a specialized third party. Becoming a certified B-Corp shows transparency and a serious commitment to the company's environmental and social activities. Additionally, certification can open the door to more investors, special discounts, and services only accessible to the certified companies. However, the certification process is rigorous, expensive, and not required by law. Additionally, the certification only lasts two years, so the company will have to pay the renewal fee, restart and pass the assessment to keep their certification every two years.

2. Low-Profit LLC (L3C)

This is a new alternative LLC model that is only available in a handful of states. L3Cs are designed to have a charitable mission while having the freedom to distribute the business's profits to its owners. L3Cs are also designed to accept investments from private investors and charitable foundations. For tax purposes, foundations can only invest in a for-profit company if it qualifies as a program-related investment (PRI). Qualifying as a PRI requires the investment to further the foundation's charitable mission. So the PRI cannot be made for the sole purpose of monetary return, or in support of lobbying or political campaigns. However, becoming an L3C will not guarantee you will qualify as a PRI for a particular foundation, and the government requires an L3C to follow additional regulations to maintain their low-profit status.

3. **Flexible Purpose Corporations**

    This is one of the newest types of business forms, and as of 2015, California is the only state that recognizes FPCs as a corporate form. FPCs protect executives from unprofitable business decisions related to the FCP's chosen public purpose, which can be anything, as long as it is for the public good. What differentiates FPCs from B-Corps and L3Cs is that an existing corporation, partnership, or LLC in California can convert to an FPC through a shareholder vote at any time. Additionally, the name of the FPC must contain the phrase "Flexible Purpose Corporation" or the abbreviation FPC. The advantages of choosing the FPC model in California include the ability to focus on short-term benefits for employees, the community, or the environment, and the ability to switch back to a traditional entity when the FPC completes its objective. On the down side, there are no tax benefits and you must maintain the formalities of your original corporate form.

4. **Cooperatives**

    A co-op is a business model that allows a group of people to come together to contribute their individual services to a general goal. Members buy-in to the co-op by paying a fee or other contribution, which the co-op then uses as capital. Usually, the members elect a board of directors that will be responsible for governing the co-op, and a staff to make the day-to-day decisions. Profits are referred to as surplus and can be distributed to the members based on their contribution at the end of the year. Co-ops can deduct any member payout from their taxes as a corporation, so in a way they are tax-exempt. However, members will pay the taxes based on their payout from the co-op.

Choosing the appropriate business model can be tricky because every project has different needs. The best way to nurture your project and avoid a confusing legal mess is to work with an attorney from the beginning. Business needs evolve over time, so be open to consulting with other professionals along the way to help you deal with tax, employment, and liability issues as they arise. When the time is right, and you've worked with an attorney and other business professionals to put the pieces together, your business will be able to thrive.

Chapter 2
Intellectual Property 101:
Patenting Your Book, Trademarking Your Invention and Other IP Mistakes to Avoid

Many types of creative and technical content are protected by one of the four types of Intellectual Property Law: copyright, trademark, patent, and trade secret. Unlike real property law, which governs physical property and land, Intellectual Property governs the use of creative and technical works as well as brands. Whether you're reusing content or trying to protect your content and ideas, it's critical that you understand which types of Intellectual Property might be in play. In this chapter we break down the 4 main types of Intellectual Property and explain: what they protect; how protection is granted; if registration is required, when you should apply for it, and if you'll need help from an attorney; how long that protection lasts; what rights you are granted.

Copyright

THE BOTTOM LINE

Copyright law protects your creative expression (but not your ideas!) for a very, very long time.

What does copyright law protect?

Copyright protects creative expression that has been fixed in a tangible medium of expression. So what does that mean when translated from legalese? It means copyright protects most creative content you create that has been written down or recorded. Copyright protects things like books, movies, songs, drawings, photographs, software code, and emails. Also it's important to know that the bar for creativity is very low. How low? If your book is even slightly more creative than a strictly alphabetical phonebook, it's probably protected. But that doesn't mean that copyright protects everything, so here are a few very important exceptions to know about:

- **Copyright does not protect ideas.**

  While copyright does protect creative expression, it doesn't protect the ideas behind them. So while you couldn't take the original *Star Wars* script and film your own version of the movie, you could write your own space opera with a hero narrative and film it, because space operas and hero narratives are ideas.

- **Copyright does not protect names, titles, numbers, short phrases, or slogans.**

- **Copyright does not protect public domain works.**

  Although copyright lasts a very long time, it doesn't last forever. Once the copyright term has expired on a work, it enters the public domain and is free to use.

How is copyright protection granted?

Copyright is automatically granted from the moment you create your expression. The moment you save that screenplay, take a selfie, or record your next hit single; your creative work is protected. This also means that when you create a work with other people, if you don't have an agreement to the contrary, you likely all share ownership of the copyright to the work.

While the US Copyright Office does allow you to register your copyright, it is not necessary to register your copyright to get protection. However, prompt copyright registration can afford you certain benefits like statutory damages and attorney's fees if you ever need to go to court to enforce your copyright.

Putting the copyright symbol or a watermark on your work is also not required for copyright protection. However, putting the copyright symbol next to your work can be practical way to clarify to the public that you own the copyrighted work, particularly if you release your work online.
Trust us, if we had a nickel for every time someone told us "but it didn't have a copyright symbol, so it can't be protected by copyright" we would have a sled worthy mountain of nickels.

When should you register for copyright protection?

From a practical perspective, it may be difficult to find an attorney to take your copyright case unless you registered before someone copied (infringed) your work without permission. Prompt registration means that significant statutory damages and attorney's fees could be available, and your case could be much more attractive to an attorney. While there are some attorneys who will take copyright cases "on contingency," meaning you pay little or nothing upfront and they take a share of the damages award if you win, these attorneys tend to be few and far between. Otherwise you'll need to be independently wealthy and able pay your attorney's fees upfront and out of pocket. This means that you need to consider early on whether registration is right for you. Anytime you have a work that you think will be valuable in the future, or that has clearly shown value, it's probably time to go ahead and register that work.

It's not always an easy choice if you're a blogger or video creator creating many works per week, so you'll want to think carefully about which works are worth it for you to register.

Can you register for copyright protection on your own, or do you need a lawyer for that?

While there are lawyers that can help you register your work for copyright protection, in many cases you can register for protection yourself. The Copyright Office even has an online registration process[7] that is faster and less expensive than the old paper process. You'll need to answer a series of questions on multiple screens as accurately and completely as possible. However, for musical works, works with more than one creator, computer code or a large number of works, things get complicated pretty quickly and you may want to reach out and get help from an attorney.

How long does copyright protection last?

Copyright protection lasts a very long time. Most works created after 1978 are protected by copyright for the life of the creator plus 70 years. But anything created before 1978 will have a different copyright life span, depending on when it was created. Check out this useful chart on copyright duration for more specific details.[8]

What rights do copyright owners have?

Copyright law grants copyright owners six exclusive rights: (1) to reproduce (aka make copies of) the copyrighted work; (2) to prepare new versions and adaptations of your original copyrighted work (this is also known as

---

7   "ECO Registration System." U. S. Copyright Office. Web. 23 Feb. 2016. <http://copyright.gov/eco/>.
8   "Copyright Term and the Public Domain in the United States." Cornell Copyright Information Center. Web. 23 Feb. 2016. <http://copyright.cornell.edu/resources/publicdomain.cfm>.

the derivative work right); (3) to publicly distribute the copyrighted work; (4) to publicly perform the copyrighted work; (5) to publicly display the copyrighted work; and (6) to digitally perform copyrighted sound recordings.

Only the copyright owner can authorize these types of uses. Keep in mind that person who originally created a work, such as an author, filmmaker, or musician, may not be actually the copyright owner (for example, a record company or movie studio might own the work instead). The copyright owner can assign, transfer, license or otherwise contract away their rights. So when you're looking to get permission to use one of these rights, make sure you get written permission (for more on getting permission the right way, see Chapter 8) from the copyright owner!

Trademark

THE BOTTOM LINE

Trademark can protect your brand, logo or slogans but unlike copyright it takes some work to get these rights.
Remember trademark law's primary purpose is to protect consumers from confusion.Carefully choose your trademark, because there's nothing worse than building up a bunch of good will in a trademark someone else was already using!

What do trademarks protect?

Trademark law is intended to protect consumers from confusion related to a product or service's origin. Essentially, when a customer picks up a can of Coca-Cola, trademark law ensures that they're getting actual Coca-Cola instead of water with brown food dye. But trademark protects more than just names; it also protects logos, emblems, and characters. Trademark law also protects "trade dress," which is separate from logos and symbols, and protects the physical appearance of the product or service. For example, trade dress may cover the shape, look and feel, or color scheme of a product if it is associated with a specific company.

How is trademark protection granted?

To have a trademark, you typically first need to use whatever mark you're trying to gain protection on in relation to the sale of goods or services. From there you have two options (1) continue to use the mark as a way of getting trademark protection (common law protection), or (2) formally apply for trademark protection at the US Trademark Office. Since registering your trademark costs money and will likely require hiring an attorney it's important to know what the benefits of registration are. Here are the top three benefits:

- **National Protection**

  Without a federal registration, you only get trademark protection in the specific geographic areas you sell your good or service. This can be particularly important for online creators who need national protection and don't want to prove all of the places their goods or services are sold.

- **Proof that the mark is yours**

  By registering the mark, you get an official government record that says that you are the owner of the mark and when you started using it. This can come in handy if you ever get sued and need to prove that you own the mark.

- **Easier Licensing**

  It is much easier to draft a license for others to use your trademark if it is registered. It also helps assure those wishing to license your trademark that it actually belongs to you.

When should you register your Trademark?

You should register your trademark as soon as you start selling the product although you can also file an "intent to use" trademark application to reserve the mark before you start selling your good or service. Keep in mind registration can take awhile, so it's better to start the registration process sooner rather than later. Certain steps of the process, like searching to make sure no one else has trademarked that name or is already using it, should be done as soon as you have an idea of what you'd like to trademark. There's nothing worse than building up months of goodwill, then getting a nastygram on the day before you launch letting you know that the name is already in use and you have to stop selling your product.

Can you register for trademark protection on your own, or do you need a lawyer for that?

You should always have an attorney register your trademark. An experienced trademark attorney can do a more thorough trademark search to make sure your mark can be registered, and can help you clearly identify the types of services the mark protects. Using a trademark attorney up front means (1) fewer disputes down the road, (2) an easier path to getting registered, and (3) a greater chance you'll win disputes down the road.

How long does Trademark protection last?

If you don't register your trademark your trademark protection can last indefinitely provided that (1) you're still using it on your products or services, (2) it doesn't become generic, and (3) no one else using it challenges your mark.

If you do register your mark your trademark protection can also last indefinitely provided that (1) you're still using it, (2) it doesn't become generic, (3) no one else using it challenges your mark, AND (4) you renew your trademark every 10 years.

What rights do trademark owners get?

Trademark gives you the exclusive right to use your mark in connection with a very specific set of goods or services either based on your current use or the categories in which you register your trademark. For example, let's say you register the term Hipster Owl for your band. Depending on how you registered the mark, you would likely be able to use Hipster Owl in connection with your band and your merchandise. But let's say an entrepreneur wanted to name their restaurant Hipster Owl Ramen Shop. Your trademark likely would not prevent them from opening the ramen shop because they are in a completely different category of business. It also seems unlikely that someone would confuse a band with a ramen shop.

Patents

What do patents protect?

A patent is a form of intellectual property that protects leaps of invention that are (1) new, (2) useful, and (3) non-obvious. Leaps of invention that have been protected by patent law have included everything from over-the-counter medications like acetaminophen, to certain types of software and even Edison's light bulb.

How is patent protection granted?

In order to qualify for patent protection, the inventor (or someone they've given their patent rights to) must register the patent with the US Patent and Trademark Office. For more information about how to register a patent, you can visit the visit US Patent and Trademark Office website here.[9]

When should your register for patent protection?

You should register your patent as soon as you can afford to. Under the America Invents Act, the US became a "first to file" country. That means whomever registers the patent first gets the patent, even if someone else came up with the invention first. Another thing to keep in mind is that in some countries, if you publicly disclose your idea before filing for a patent you lose the ability to patent your invention in that country. The US is a bit more lax in that you get a one year window from publicly disclosing your idea to register. However, even with the one year window, if someone registers your idea before you do, they still get the patent.

---

9   United States Patent and Trademark Office. Web. 23 Feb. 2016.
     <http://www.uspto.gov/>.

Can you register for patent protection on your own, or do you need a lawyer for that?

You should always work with a patent attorney or registered patent agent to register your patent. Writing a patent can be complicated, particularly if you'd like to patent something related to software. Using a patent attorney up front means an easier path to getting registered, and a greater chance you'll win disputes down the road. In fact, because the US Patent Office thinks it's critical that inventors work with attorneys, they've developed a host of programs to help inventors to connect with free or low cost patent attorneys. You can find out more about those programs here.[10]

How long does patent protection last?

Once the patent has been registered with the US Patent and Trademark Office, the patent will last for 20 years. However, extensions are possible and foreign patents might have different patent terms.

What rights is the patent owner granted?

The patent owner is granted the right to prevent others from making, using, or selling their patented invention without permission.

Trade Secret

THE BOTTOM LINE

Trade secrets can protect a wide variety of things – as long as you can keep them a secret.

What do trade secrets protect?

Trade secrets can protect anything that derives its value from being secret. Things like the Coca-Cola recipe, a marketing strategy, or even a computer algorithm can be trade secrets.

10 "Using Legal Services." United States Patent and Trademark Office. Web. 23 Feb. 2016. <http://www.uspto.gov/patents-getting-started/using-legal-services>.

How is trade secret protection granted?

You can get trade secret protection by keeping something a secret. But a pinky swear isn't going to cut it. When it comes to protecting your trade secrets, not only should you have Non-Disclosure Agreements (for more on Non-Disclosure Agreements see Chapter 4) and written practices for keeping your material secret, but you also actually have to follow through on those practices. For example, let's say one of your practices for keeping your secret formula confidential is that the secret formula cannot leave the company vault, employees must sign in before entering the vault, and they may not bring anything into the vault with them when they look at the formula. If you start allowing employees to enter the vault without signing in and allow them to take the formula back to their desk or even outside the office, there's a good chance that even if you had all of your employees sign NDA's, your Trade secret would no longer be considered a protectable trade secret by a court. Also if something is public knowledge it can't be a trade secret. So if the thing that you'd like to protect can be found via a Google search, it's not a trade secret.

Can I protect a trade secret on my own or do I need a lawyer for that?

While there's no process for "registering" a trade secret, a trade secret lawyer can help you figure out the kind of business practices that are necessary to getting and keeping trade secret protection. This includes everything from suggesting the best means of securing your trade secret, to drafting employee handbooks and agreements that ensure your employees understand their responsibility to protect trade secrets.

How long does trade secret protection last?

Trade secret protection lasts as long as you can keep your secret a secret. However, if you fail to keep it a secret inadvertently (as described above) or if your secret is publicly disclosed, you may lose your trade secret protection. So what counts as "public disclosure?" Generally, if your secret is independently published by third parties, becomes common knowledge within your industry, or is publicly disclosed by you, this counts as public disclosure and could eliminate your trade secret protection.

What rights are you granted under trade secret law?

Trade secret law is a bit different than other types of IP law, because it really only protects people who know your secret from making that public. It doesn't prevent others from going off and creating the exact same thing or something very similar. So trade secret enforcement is really all about stopping the harm of having your secrets shared. This typically means going to a court to ask them to stop the other person from using or sharing your trade secret (this is known as an injunction) or asking that the other person pay for what they did through monetary damages. Certain trade secret violations can even bring jail time.

As you can see, the four types of Intellectual Property Law all serve very different purposes. By knowing the difference between them, you'll not only be more interesting at dinner parties, but you'll also be better able to protect your work and understand how you can legally reuse the work of others.

Chapter 3
How to Know if They're an Employee
or an Independent Contractor

THE BOTTOM LINE

When you pay another creator to work for you, you should be careful about whether you classify them as an employee or an independent contractor. Simply writing up a contract that says someone is an independent contractor does not make it so in the eyes of the IRS.

An individual's classification can have important consequences for your business, especially regarding the ownership of what your business creates. While you generally own what employees create, you don't own what an independent contractor creates without a written agreement.

So you want to work with someone on a book, film, song, game, software, or other creative project? Most creators and entrepreneurs realize early on that they can't do it all. For your project to really take off, you will need to work with individuals that can bring a variety of creative, technical, marketing, financial, and other expertise to your project.

You may not realize it, but your contract software developer, songwriting partner, illustrator, or your regular writing collaborator may all create complex intellectual property and legal liability issues for you.
The good news is that these issues can be addressed relatively painlessly by establishing some expectations at the outset of your business relationships with independent contractors. Addressing problems up front beats leaving things unclear and waiting for disaster any day.

This chapter will give an overview of what to think about when you're considering whether to work with someone as an employee or independent contractor. We'll discuss the benefits, challenges, and limitations to each path. We'll also offer some best practices to keep everyone working on your projects, rather than stuck in legal disputes.

They're either an employee or an independent contractor

There are two ways you can pay those you hire, either as employees or as independent contractors. Startups and small companies are sometimes hesitant to hire employees because employees are expensive, and require quite a bit of additional administrative work. You have to withhold the taxes, pay unemployment insurance, pay workers' comp, make sure they get their breaks, post that weird convoluted poster in the break room, and conform to Occupational Safety & Health Administration's standards, to name a few. You may think, "why not just call everyone I pay an independent contractor and call it a day?" Well, it's not that easy

Independent contractor status is hard to get and hard to keep. So let's talk about who is an employee, who is an independent contractor, and the steps you can take when you hire people as independent contractors to ensure they don't become a surprise employee. A surprise employee could sue you for back wages, among other things, and also get you in trouble with the IRS.

Who is an employee, and who is an independent contractor?

Employees

When does a worker qualify as an employee?

Employees are people you pay to work under your control. You provide them with a goal and the exact details of how you want them to reach that goal, while generally overseeing the process. If you provide a space for them to work, the equipment to do the work, or schedule the hours that someone will work, that person may be considered an employee.

The benefits of hiring employees.

One benefit of having employees is that the work they do for you is generally considered a "work for hire", that means you automatically own the work they do for you. If you want to retain ownership, it's still a good idea to clarify that you or your company will own anything the employee creates in your employment agreement and personnel handbook. In general, you're in a much better position to claim ownership with an employee than with an independent contractor. You also have more control over how the employee does their work.

Employer duties towards their employees.

Employers need to pay benefits, insurance, taxes, worker's comp, meet OSHA standards, make sure employees take appropriate breaks, and make sure that weird labor law poster is displayed in the break room, among other requirements.

There are serious consequences when an employer doesn't fulfill these duties.

If you don't follow the rules set out for properly having employees, and say, misclassify an employee as an independent contractor; that individual could come back and sue you later for back pay, which would likely tank any project you have going on. Did we mention the IRS?

Independent Contractors

When a worker qualifies as an independent contractor.

Independent contractors are people you pay, over whom you do not take the same kind of financial or behavioral control as employees. The big difference between independent contractors and employees is the level of control that you have over the person working for you. You provide them with the deliverables for a project, but it's mostly up to them to figure out the details of how to get the project completed. If you're pretty hands-off about the work the person you hired is doing, that person will probably be considered an IC. If you have control over every part of what the person is doing, that person is probably an employee. Here are some examples:

- **Good example of an independent contractor.**

  Let's say you find an artist on Deviant Art to do some graphic design work for you. You offer to pay her a fixed amount of money for three images. After that, you don't ever talk to her again until she sends you the final images. The images look great, so you send her the money and don't talk again until you're working on your next project. This artist is a good example of an independent contractor. This is because you didn't control what she was doing at all. You just gave her a task to make some artwork for you and then she decided where she was going to work on it, what schedule she was going to keep, and just how she wanted to make the art for you.

24

- **Bad example of an independent contractor.**

  Let's say you find a local artist on Craigslist to work for your graphic design company. You rent a small office, and you require the artist to come into the office everyday so you can oversee her work on the images. You tell her she can't work on the art after hours because all the changes she does after hours when you're not there confuse you. You tell her that she can't do work for anyone else, because you want her to concentrate fully on her work for your company. She's not working on a discrete project, just a continuous flow of work that you assign and oversee. Every day, you two have a meeting about how her work is going. For all these reasons, this person is almost certainly an employee, not an independent contractor.

Employer duties towards their independent contractors and what you can do to make sure the person you hired remains an independent contractor.

Simply having an individual sign an agreement saying they are an independent contractor is not enough to ensure their status and avoid a surprise employee. Courts and the IRS make it clear that what you put in an agreement is less important than how you actually behave. Here are five tips to ensure that the people you hire are really independent contractors. This is not an exhaustive list, but the more of these tips you follow, the less likely you'll run into problems.

1. **Independent contractors should use their own tools when possible.**

   If they can work on their own laptops and other equipment, it would be better than providing computers for everyone.

2. **Independent contractors should be allowed to work at their own location.**

   If their job directly requires them being somewhere specific, then disregard this tip. Just know, however, that if there are parts of the person's tasks that can be done in ANY location, you should at least give that person the choice of doing it wherever he or she likes.

3. **Try to be a little hands-off about the manner in which people get a task done.**

   If you require everyone to work on Macs because that's the only way your software runs, that makes sense. But if you force someone to get a Mac just because you're their boss and you hate PCs, then your heavy handedness might bring you closer to employer territory.

You can definitely make people work within specifications, but as long as the person has a way of creating the product within those specs, don't be too controlling about the manner in which the person does it.

4. **If you do have employees, don't have your independent contractor doing the same or similar tasks as your employees.**

   In fact, don't do anything that makes them seem like employees if you don't have to. For example, if you have a lead artist and a junior artist employee working with you, don't give the independent contractor the title of junior artist. Maybe add the word "consultant" to the person's title to make things clear. If the person is working on the project for a very short time, maybe allow them to use their own email address instead of a company email. Only let them attend staff meetings that are relevant to their job or not at all.

5. **Pay independent contractors per project, and try to avoid paying them hourly or a fixed yearly salary, if possible.**

The benefits of hiring independent contractors.

The benefits of an independent contractor are that you don't have to pay for and administrate their benefits, insurances, taxes, and you're not responsible for the employment laws we discussed earlier for employees.

There are serious consequences when an employer doesn't fulfill these duties.

Why does it matter where someone works or whose computer they do their work on? If the people working with you get mad at you, they can come back later and sue you for back pay, other benefits, and in some states, triple the amount that they would've earned if they were classified correctly. Oh and did we mention the IRS?

Even if you think no one will sue you because you're friends, sometimes bad or unexpected things happen and people need money. Babies arrive, investments fail, the house gets burned down without insurance...stuff happens. There are lawyers who make their entire livings convincing people, like your friends, to sue their former employers. You don't want to be one of those employers.

Of course, employees are misclassified as independent contractors all the time and nobody ever gets in trouble or gets sued. In fact, there may be more independent contractors working right now who are misclassified than independent contractors who are classified correctly. However, "they were doing it too" has and never will be a legal defense. The point is, if you can follow any of the tips above easily, and you take a little time to learn a bit more about the independent contractor laws, you could save yourself months of future hassle.

Make sure you own what your independent contractor is creating!

A key difference with independent contractors from employees is that you have to get an agreement in place if you want to own the things you're paying them to create. You need to have an agreement in place (preferably before work starts) where they assign all their rights to the work they're about to do for you to you. In some cases a work-for-hire agreement may be appropriate, which is slightly different than an assignment, and allows you to own the rights immediately rather than needing an assignment. If you don't have an assignment or work-for-hire in place, then you don't own the copyright to the work, and the independent contractor could legally keep it for themselves or (more nefariously) require you pay them more to own or use the rights. If you choose to not to get the work assigned to you for some reason, make sure to get a broad enough license to use what the contractor creates in the way you intended. Remember also that if you don't get an assignment, you may not have the ability to enforce your rights against others down the line.

Here are two more things you should know about assignment agreements:

- **It's best to get this assignment agreement signed before the IC does any work.**

   Of course it can be signed at any time, even after the work has been completed. But if they don't sign it when they start working, you run the risk of them not wanting to sign it later. Occasionally, contractors can completely disappear on you, so you should secure the rights early.

- **Assignment agreements MUST be made in writing.**

   They can't be made orally. If you've already hired someone without an assignment or a contract to do work for you, and you're worried about your rights and who owns what, you should talk to an attorney.

Hopefully this provides you with some background on how to walk the line between independent contractors and employees. If you are trying to figure out how to hire and classify your workers, we highly recommend contacting an attorney in your state to make sure you've met all applicable state and federal requirements.

Chapter 4
Keeping it Confidential: Some FAQ's About NDA's

What is an NDA?

An NDA is a legal contract that lays out particular material, knowledge or information that two parties want to share with each other, but not with others.

When might I need an NDA?

NDAs are used when you want to confidentially share information with other parties. They are usually used to protect information that is valuable but not protected under patent, copyright or trademark law. An example of a common use of an NDA would be when you have an idea to share that might be protected by patent law, but you haven't had a chance to file your patent yet.

Can't I just use this NDA I found on the internet?

You can….but it's not a good idea. The random NDA you found out in the wilds of the internet won't necessarily be enforceable or helpful to you in the long run. To be enforceable, an NDA must address:

• What specific types of information are being shared.

28

- Why the information is being shared.

- What both parties can specifically do with the information.

- And otherwise meet all the other requirements for a valid contract.

To ensure that the purpose of the NDA and the promises made in the agreement are specific enough to hold up, it can often be a good idea to work with an attorney on your NDA. Some attorneys may even be willing to draft templates for you that are tailored to your needs, but that can be used in a variety of circumstances.

So once I've got an NDA I'm good, right?

Not necessarily. If your NDA protects information that is a trade secret, having a nice piece of paper saying you'll keep the information a secret just won't cut it. You actually have to take measures to keep that information secret. These practical measures could include anything from locking a secret formula in a vault, to ensuring that employees cannot plug in thumb drives on computers with secret information. Taking these practical steps will help your trade secrets stay secret (for more on trade secrets, see Chapter 2).

So I don't trust this other person at all, but if I sign an NDA it'll be ok right?

Maybe? As a general business principal, it's a bad idea to work with people you don't trust even a little bit and hope for the best. No piece of paper can stop someone from doing something, like sharing all of your information, if they really want to. A good contract *can* provide some serious legal consequences to help you mitigate the damages. But it's often more efficient to not enter into a relationship with an untrustworthy person than to enter into one and have to sue them later.

Chapter 5
Insurance: Do I Need it and What Does it Do?

THE BOTTOM LINE

This chapter provides a general overview of the different types of insurance policies available to small businesses and startup companies. You always want to work closely with an insurance company or broker to understand the specifics of every policy that you pay for, so you can understand exactly what is and is not covered.

Also, don't assume that your insurance needs in the first year will continue to cover you after you have three more years of growth, six new employees, and a storage unit full of expensive equipment. You don't want to be blindsided by big out-of-pocket expenses that you thought you were protected against.

New technologies and new laws may also pave the way for new insurance requirements. Work closely with your insurance provider(s), checking in periodically to ensure that you and all of your assets are always adequately protected.

It can be difficult to understand all the different types of insurance, and determine what your business needs. This chapter is about the variety of business insurance policies that are available on the marketplace. It should help you understand the basics about the variety of policies; what each of them cover; and when and why you should consider each type for your small business or tech startup.

Choose your insurance broker or agent carefully!

First things first: it is important to develop a good working relationship with a respectable insurance company. Your insurance company and agent should be available and willing to answer all of the many questions that you will undoubtedly have for them. Insurance policies may differ slightly among the many providers, and it's important that you understand exactly what you are getting, as well as what you're not getting, when you purchase a policy.

Remember that you have options when it comes to insurance. You should work with a respectable and helpful insurance agent who understands your needs and concerns, and can communicate what the insurance company expects of you. The agent should be able to recommend policies that provide protection based on your specific needs. Ask questions, shop around, and read your policies to understand what is and isn't covered. Below are the key types of insurance that you may need for your business:

- Professional Liability

- General Liability

- Commercial Property

- Homeowner's and Renter's

- Business Interruption

- Cyber Liability

- Commercial Auto Liability

- Product Liability

- Directors and Officers

- Key Person

- Business Owners

- Worker's Compensation

- Health

Professional Liability —
Errors & Omissions Insurance: When Mistakes Cost Big Bucks.

Professional liability insurance, also known as "errors and omissions insurance" (E&O insurance), will help protect your assets against claims of negligence, misrepresentation, and inaccurate advice. Essentially, an E&O policy will back you up when you make a mistake or an error that ends up costing a lot of money. Some professionals, such as lawyers, doctors, and accountants, are actually required to have a professional liability policy. Others, like filmmakers, need to have E&O insurance if they want to distribute outside of YouTube and Facebook, on platforms such as on Netflix, Hulu or HBO.

Even if your particular industry doesn't require E&O insurance, it may still be worth considering purchasing. For example, if you provide a service or software that your clients rely on heavily to do business or manage data, or if you produce any kind of creative work that reuses anyone else's work without permission, then you will want to consider purchasing E&O insurance.

E&O Insurance in general: How is it different from General Liability Insurance?

It's important to understand that professional liability insurance is not the same as general liability insurance. A general liability policy, discussed in more detail later on, covers claims made for damage to a person or to physical property. A typical E&O policy, however, protects claims made for damages (the legal term for money) for things such as intellectual property infringement, data breaches, reputation, and other forms of intangible property. This can be particularly important for technology and creative ventures that are often highly reliant on intangible property in their business.

For example, if your tech startup provides a digital platform for companies to collect customer orders and that platform goes down for a week, your clients are going to lose business opportunities. They may sue you because you promised to provide their business platform and then failed to do so. Hopefully you accounted for this with a well-drafted terms of use, but this is where your E&O policy might come into play to help cover their claim against you for lost profits.

On the creative side, maybe you just finished your first documentary film and a large media company claims that you used content that infringes on some creative material they own that's protected by copyright.

Your E&O policy may help you defend against such a lawsuit. Even if the claim is found to be groundless because you did your due diligence and made sure to get permission or a fair use opinion on everything you reused, it could still end up costing you a lot of money to defend yourself. Without an E&O policy, you are putting yourself at risk of having to cover all of those costs.

E&O Policies only cover claims when the policy is active

Professional liability insurance also differs from general liability insurance in the timing of claims. Most general liability policies cover claims that allegedly occurred while the policy was in place, even if the actual claim comes years later and you have since cancelled or changed policies. As long as the policy was active at the time that the wrongful act allegedly occurred, your policy will provide protection. Professional liability works a bit differently. E&O claims can only be protected with insurance when the actual policy is active. Once you let your E&O policy lapse or you cancel coverage, you are no longer protected against claims of mistake or error, even if it allegedly occurred while your policy was in place. This means that even if you close down your business or go inactive for a period of time, you may still be at risk of claims from former clients. Make sure you communicate closely with your insurance agent before you cancel your E&O policy.

The different types of E&O

Different industries have different standards and types of E&O insurance policies and requirements. Here are a few different specific options for small businesses and startups in the creative and technology fields that we've addressed below.

1. **Producer's E&O Insurance**

   Producer's E&O insurance protects a piece of media from claims of copyright infringement, libel, slander, plagiarism, among other things. As we've mentioned, you typically need Producer's E&O Insurance before distribution. This is because many distribution companies will often not work with a film, TV show, or radio show until the producer has acquired an E&O policy that protects that particular piece of media. To get an E&O policy on your film or show, you must work with a licensed attorney first. The attorney will review the film, informing you if any parts of it are at risk for lawsuits. You will then have the opportunity to make changes and adjust the film before seeking an E&O policy from an insurance agent. Once your edits are cleared by the attorney, he or she will write a letter to the insurance company with his or her professional opinion about your film. The insurance agency pays particular attention to the attorney's opinion when deciding whether to offer you a policy and how much to charge you. This process may take a few days or a few months, depending on the content of your film and how quickly you can make edits. It's important to be as accurate and complete with your attorney as possible.

Be sure to work with an attorney as soon as possible, preferably right as pre-production begins. Because many E&O policies contain "Clearance Procedures" that require an attorney to be involved from the outset of a production. The earlier you reach out to an attorney, the easier your path to getting insurance will be.

2. Media Peril E&O Insurance (aka "Media Liability Insurance")

Media Peril E&O insurance is for authors, bloggers, and freelance writers. It is similar to a producer's E&O policy in that it protects an author from the costs associated with defending claims of copyright infringement, libel, and invasion of privacy. The policy may also help you pay out any judgments or settlements that are reached as a result of claims against your written work. Once your work is made public, it can reach many people very quickly; it's best to have a policy in place before you publish or post your work publicly. You can get a policy as an individual or as a business entity. Depending on whether you write casually as a blogger or more full-time as an author, you should work with your insurance agent to determine if your particular situation warrants an individual policy or a business policy.

3. Tech E&O Insurance

Tech E&O insurance covers a broad range of technology based business liabilities. It is intended for the types of companies who do things like create component parts for computers or robots, develop software and apps, or consult with companies about their technology systems and options. A tech E&O policy can help cover costs associated with claims that a product doesn't work the way you promised it would. Those customers could try to sue you to cover the costs associated with rectifying the problem, and without an E&O policy, those claims could cost you thousands of dollars you don't have yet. It is best to be covered for these possible errors before you start providing services to your clients.

Even if you don't seem to fit into any of the three categories above, you should still consider an E&O policy if you provide services that could lead to intangible claims.

While professional liability insurance is arguably the most important type of insurance for creators and entrepreneurs, it does not protect against every situation. There are a variety of other insurance types that you should consider and reconsider as your company grows.

General Liability Insurance: Basic Coverage for Basic Injury

A general liability policy protects you from claims of bodily injury or property damage. For example, if your new employee hits a mailbox after delivering a product to your customer, your general liability policy will cover the cost of replacing their mailbox so you don't have to pay out of company profits or your own pocket. General liability insurance may also cover costs associated with medical bills from a client who walks into your office and trips on a loose computer cord. If you and your employees routinely interact physically with customers, whether you are making deliveries to them or you have an open storefront where your customers come to you, it is best to have a general liability policy to cover costs associated with any accident that involves those customers or their property. General liability insurance is also commonly bundled into a business owner's policy, also discussed in more detail below.

General Liability insurance does not cover identity and privacy claims

General liability coverage typically will not protect you against any harm to intangible property, such as a person's identity or personal information. Almost all companies store customer information electronically; the common way to protect against liability for breaches of that information is a cyber liability policy, discussed below.

A general liability policy will cover harms that occur during your coverage period, even if the accusation comes many years later, and you have since terminated the policy. This is very different from a professional liability policy, which only covers claims that are actually made during the policy term.

Commercial Property Insurance: Protection for the Bones of your Business

Commercial property insurance will cover the costs associated with replacing damaged business property and equipment. Damage to your business property may come from things like fire, theft, and vandalism. To be protected from floods and earthquakes, you may need to add additional coverage, so check with your insurance provider. This is the broadest form of protection for your business property, and comes into play after your homegrown startup has outgrown its in-home business insurance coverage provided by most homeowner's insurance policies. Commercial property insurance is commonly bundled into a business owner's policy, discussed in more detail below. See the section on homeowner's and renter's insurance for alternative, inexpensive coverage options to insure your in-home business equipment.

Homeowner's and Renter's Insurance:
Minimal Protection for your Home-Based Business

If you are working from the comfort of home, your typical homeowner's or renter's policy could leave you high and dry in the event of damage or theft to your business supplies and equipment. Most homeowner's and renter's policies will not cover costs associated with damage to your business equipment, even if that equipment lives under the same roof that you do.

When do you add Home-Based Business Insurance?

You'll have to make this call by weighing the cost of additional coverage against the potential loss from theft or damage of your business equipment. The first thing you should do is to try calling your existing homeowner's insurance provider and ask about available options to protect your business assets. Sometimes, the least expensive and easiest option is to add a "rider" to your existing policy. The rider would be a small extension of coverage to include what little office equipment your company currently uses. As your company grows and equipment values increase, your insurance coverage should increase as well. When your assets have outgrown your rider, reach back out to your provider and discuss trading out that rider for an in-home business policy. The in-home business policy will cost a little more each month, but will provide greater protection for your upgraded assets.

What comes after I've outgrown my Home-Based Business Insurance?

When you've outgrown your maximum coverage on an in-home business policy, you'll want to split up your homeowner's policy and your business policy. This way, your homeowner's or renter's insurance can go back to protecting only your personal belongings, and your business belongings will be protected by a commercial property insurance policy. This type of coverage will cost you the most, but it will also provide the broadest form of protection.

Business Interruption Insurance: Keep Going When the Going Gets Tough

A typical business interruption policy will cover the costs associated with keeping your business functioning when you suffer from an incident that could stall production or prevent you from connecting with customers. Business interruption insurance requires documentation of your monthly net profits, so if you run a startup that is growing quickly, you will want to carefully document that growth. If you need to use your business interruption insurance, you will want to be covered for the next month's projected increased profits, not last month's lower profit figure. A typical business interruption policy will cover tangible property losses in the wake of a disaster, as well as business expenses such as payroll costs that may become difficult to cover after a disruption in operations. For example, if a fire destroys your storage unit full of computer parts, you will be unable to bring in revenue for a little while as you build and prepare new parts. A business interruption policy can help both with the costs of obtaining these new parts as well as covering employee payroll during this downtime. But, be aware! For protection after a flood, you will likely have to add that protection to the policy, just like you do on your homeowner's policy, so talk to your insurance provider if you are concerned about a flood disrupting your business. When your business operating costs become so expensive that an interruption in revenue would mean you cannot cover those costs, you will want to look into a business interruption policy. Business interruption insurance is commonly bundled into a business owner's policy, discussed in more detail below.

Cyber Liability Insurance: Protection from the Dreaded Data Breach

A typical general liability policy will not cover a breach in company and customer data. That's where cyber liability insurance comes in. If your data, including the personal information of your customers, becomes compromised and you are not covered under a cyber liability policy, the costs associated with defending and rectifying the breach could result in very expensive bills. This type of insurance is especially worth considering if you collect a lot of personal information from your customers, including location data, credit card numbers, addresses, and other personal information. Different states have different requirements for how a company must handle a data breach, such as when and how to notify individuals whose personal information may have gotten into the hands of unauthorized third parties. Cyber liability insurance may cover costs associated with following state regulations for dealing with a data breach, and costs associated with defending a lawsuit from individuals whose information was compromised because of your data breach. Make sure to talk with your provider so you know exactly what (defense of a lawsuit and/or costs of complying with state regulations) your plan will and will not cover.

Commercial Auto Insurance: Protection for Both you and your Employees

A commercial auto insurance policy covers a variety of vehicles that may be operating in a company of any size. Collision coverage in a commercial auto insurance policy covers any company vehicle for any damage caused or obtained while using the vehicle within the scope of the company's business. It doesn't matter if the driver is the owner or an employee, as long as it is a company-owned vehicle used for *business* purposes. In addition, a commercial auto insurance policy will cover any damages obtained or caused by your employees' vehicles while they are operating within the scope of their employment. This would include running company errands, transporting company employees, and could even cover damages resulting from a car accident while the employee is picking up lunch for the office. When a company purchases its own vehicles or routinely requires that employees use their own vehicles for work-related errands and travel, that company should consider adding a commercial auto insurance policy to its insurance repertoire. If your employees just commute to and from the office and take their own lunch breaks, they are covered under their own personal auto policy and there is likely no need for a commercial auto insurance policy. Commercial auto insurance can also be expanded to include comprehensive coverage, which protects business vehicles from damage from such things as hail, theft, vandalism, or fire.

Product Liability Insurance: Protection from a Potentially Faulty Product

Product liability insurance will cover your company in the event that your product causes some sort of injury or adverse reaction to the consumer. Your company should get product liability insurance as soon as it starts

creating or distributing goods that are sold to the public.
Specifically, companies selling, making, and/or distributing food items or beauty products will want to strongly consider product liability insurance. For example, if a consumer has an adverse reaction to any component of a beauty product or an allergic reaction to a food item, they may attempt to sue the company that produced that product. Product liability insurance could help protect your company and cover costs in defending such a claim.

Directors and Officers Insurance:
Protection from and for the Company Decision-Makers

Directors and officers (D&O) insurance will protect the assets of companies, as well as the personal assets of directors and officers, in the event that company decision-makers face legal action for alleged harms. For instance, if a company officer makes any promises or statements that aren't true, a company could face lawsuits from unhappy investors or others who may have relied on those statements. If you hire high-level employees from a competitor company, that competitor might make a claim against you that you hired them solely to steal proprietary information and trade secrets.

This type of insurance will cover costs associated with defending and paying settlements for those and other types of claims. Remember that many D&O policies include defense costs within the liability limit, which means that the cost of defending a dispute will reduce the amount of funds available to pay a settlement or judgment. You should consider getting a directors and officers insurance policy sooner rather than later, as you probably have one director who may be at risk – you. Many investors will require it before investing in you and top talent in the industry will be more attracted to working for you if they know that you have protection for their personal assets in the form of directors and officers insurance.

Key Person Insurance: Planning for your own worst case scenario

A typical key person policy will help keep your business going if you are unable to because of injury or death. In the unfortunate event that you, the brain of your small startup, suffer serious illness or death, the company you had created may not be able to continue to thrive without another subject-guru like yourself. If you want the company's work to continue on even if you couldn't continue with it, a key person insurance policy can help. Key person insurance will cover the business costs associated with recruiting a new key subject-matter expert to lead the company you created.

Employee Practices Liability: Protection from Employee Claims

It is common for new and small companies to hire friends.
It's important to remember, however, that those friends become employees once they are hired. And sometimes, those employees don't agree with the boss' (your!) actions. Harassment, discrimination, or wrongful termination claims can potentially bankrupt you. So it's critical to make sure your business is meeting all your requirements under the law as an employer, and that you have a clear process for bringing on new employees.
While making sure your employment practices are as fair as possible can go a long way toward protecting yourself, employee claims do happen. That's when having Employee Practices Liability Insurance to protect against such claims can come in handy. Although you can purchase this type of insurance as a standalone plan, it is typically sold in a bundle with other types of insurance, particularly as part of a business owner's policy, which we'll discuss next. Keep in mind employee practices liability plans typically don't cover punitive damages or criminal fines so making sure that you have proper hiring, firing and sexual harassment plans in place that are actually followed is critical for managing your costs and your businesses reputation.

Business Owner's Policy: Bundle and Save

A business owner's policy can be tailored to include a variety of different standard business insurance types discussed in this guide. By bundling most of your insurance needs into a business owner's policy, you will almost always end up with a lower premium than if you purchased each type a la carte. The most standard business owner's policies will include general liability, commercial property, and business interruption coverage. Talk to your insurance provider to see if you can bundle and save on your insurance policies.

Worker's Compensation Insurance: A State Requirement

Worker's compensation is required in every state for every company that hires employees. In the beginning stages of your startup, when you and maybe a co-founder are the only ones working on the project,
you probably won't need to worry about worker's compensation; but as soon as you hire even one employee (and in some states three employees), you will be required by law to have worker's compensation insurance. Worker's compensation provides coverage for medical bills and lost wages for employees who are injured on the job. In exchange, employers are

protected from most but not all potential lawsuits that an injured employee may attempt to file. For example if you were to intentionally injure one of your employees, they would likely be able to sue you and collect workers compensation.

Workers compensation insurance comes in four main varieties: self insured workers plans, group self insured plans, state plans and private insurance company plans. Under the self insured option, companies may pay all workers compensation claims out of pocket to help cut costs and incentivize safety, however, most states have very specific rules for what type of companies can participate in these types of plans. Under the group self insured plans, a group of companies may pool resources to pay workers compensation expenses out of pocket but again, most states limit what types of companies may participate in these plans. State sponsored plans are open to a wider variety of businesses and can be a lower cost alternative to a private plan. Since requirements vary by state, it is best to understand the specific laws of the state where your business operates. This website[11] provides links to information on each state's worker's compensation laws.

Health Insurance: Requirements under the Affordable Care Act

The Affordable Care Act changed the way individuals and businesses approach the topic of healthcare coverage, and requirements are state specific, depending on where you are incorporated. Most states do not mandate employer-offered health care coverage until a company employs 50 full-time employees, but it is a great benefit to attract top talent in your industry. Even if you are under 50 full-time employees, you may have other kinds of requirements in your state, such as notifying employees regarding their health insurance options and providing your employees with information on various state health insurance marketplaces.

To find out more about obtaining healthcare coverage for your small business or startup company, https://www.healthcare.gov/small-businesses/employers/ provides a good overview and a link to your state's Small Business Health Options Program (SHOP) so you can customize the right health insurance options for you and your employees.

---

11 "State Workers Compensation Sites." *State & Local Government on the Net.* Web. <http://www.statelocalgov.net/50states-workers-compensation.cfm>.

Chapter 6
Mo Money, Mo Problems: Things to Think About When Getting Funded

Many creative and entrepreneurial ventures are funded by the creators or entrepreneurs themselves (AKA "bootstrapping"). But what happens if you have very short bootstraps or you don't have any at all? You may need to turn to outside funders for help. In this chapter we'll explore some of the different types of funding that may be available to help make your dream a reality, as well as some of the pitfalls associated with outside funding.

Working with investors

For many entrepreneurs, securing an investment from venture capitalists (VCs) or angel investors is the main goal. But it isn't necessarily the right path for everyone. Here are 10 things to think about before hitting up angel investors or the VC circuit.

1. **Do you actually need the money?**

   Although money can sometimes be indicative of a business's success, whenever you get money from an investor you give up some equity and with it some control of your company. Giving up some control may be worth it, for instance, as part of the path to an IPO or acquisition, but it's something you should seriously consider before you allocate the time seeking out investors.

2. **Do you have the infrastructure to accept the money?**

   It may sound basic, but having your company set up (See Chapter 1), having a bank account for your company, and having the right legal documents drafted to accept money from investors are all crucial first steps you should have in place before you ask investors for money.

3. **Do you actually have something to pitch to investors?**

   While all great ventures start with a great idea, to get funding you'll need to be able to show you've fleshed out that idea. You'll need to be able to show your idea is a viable business with market traction. Meaning that you actually have some customers or have a working version of your technology. It's better to spend a bit more time clarifying your business, or even waiting until after its launch, before asking investors for money because you'll likely only get one chance to ask that VC for money on a particular project.

4. **Does your day job own your key IP?**

If you've started your business while working a day job, there is a chance that your day job may own all of the rights to your IP, thanks to the assignment clause in your employment agreement. Before you even start working on your project you should read through your employment agreement (the same information can also be found in your employee handbook) to make sure that what you create doesn't belong to your employer. Some agreements will allow you to own what you create outside of work under limited circumstances and these circumstances vary quite a bit based on state law. If you're not sure what you're allowed to do based on your employment agreement, you should absolutely seek legal advice before you start creating anything!

5. **Does your team own your key IP?**

If you're working with a team of creators, your team may actually own the rights to the IP you've been working on together, particularly if you don't have anything in writing. (See Chapter 3). It's a good idea to consult with an attorney before securing funding to make sure you or your company actually owns your IP.

6. **Have you made decisions about how much equity each funder will get?**

It may be helpful to think of your company as a pie. You only have so much pie to go around, so while it may be tempting to give 50% or more of your company away to get operating capital, that only leaves 50% or less of your company for your fellow founders, other investors, and for stock options for your early employees.

7. **Have you done your homework?**

You'd never go on a job interview without researching the company first, right? The same rules hold true when you're talking to VCs. Make sure that you've not only researched that specific VC but that you're also familiar with key VC terminology (like B2B and MVP) before you talk formally with VCs. Keep in mind, doing this homework can also protect you. All VCs are not created equal, and some may be better fits for your company at its current stage than others. For example some VC's may provide more mentorship for early stage companies while other VC's take a more hands off approach.

8. **Know how to pitch without giving away everything.**

   Most VCs are unwilling to sign a NDA (See Chapter 4) at the early stages because they see so many ideas on a regular basis. So how do you protect yourself? Think of your pitch as a great movie trailer. Give the VCs just enough to pique their interest, but don't give away major details about how your product works, your source code or any other proprietary information. Once the VC's get serious about your company they may be willing to sign an NDA but it will likely take a lot of pitches to get to that point.

9. **Practice, practice, practice!**

   Few of us are able to walk into a room and give a perfect presentation without practicing first. Practice your pitch for your friends and family, and at informal pitch events like 1 Million Cups. That way once you get in front of the VCs you'll be prepared.

10. **You don't need to accept your first offer.**

    As tempting as it may be to take the first offer that comes your way, remember this is a two way deal. Make sure your VC brings the type of mentorship, support or expertise you need. Also if the VC is unpleasant to work with or harasses your team, it's better to walk away before they become a major problem that owns part of your company.

11. **Remember that traditional VCs are not the be-all end-all of funding.**

    Although much of the press around funding centers on VCs, there are many other options including crowdfunding, loans, and patron websites like Patreon which will discuss more below. If you don't want to give up control or hire a lawyer to help you comply with federal and state securities laws, these other options may be a much better fit.

Other Sources of Funding

Still need funding but don't want to go with a VC? In this section we'll explore some alternate ways of funding your endeavors.

Friends and Family

While you may think that selling stock for your business to your family and friends would be an easy way to raise funds for your company, there are a host of securities laws and complex reporting requirements that are implicated any time you sell stocks, bond or any other securities. Because these regulations are so complex, we're not going to go into them in detail here. But we do want to say that you should absolutely positively speak with an experienced securities or startup attorney before you sell stock to anyone, including friends or family.

Keep in mind these regulations only apply if you're offering stock or equity to your friends and family. If your family or friends were willing to loan you money, you would not need to comply with these rules. That being said, loans between friends and family have a way of leading to disputes. If you do have a friend or family member willing to loan you money, it's a good idea to get some of the basics down in writing to help mitigate disputes later on down the line.

Crowdfunding

Maybe you struck out with investors or maybe you didn't quite reach your funding goals. Crowdfunding provides another way to raise capital to get your project off the ground. Crowdfunding websites like Kickstarter or Indiegogo allow you to raise money for your work in exchange for rewards, like early versions or your product or merchandise. This type of crowdfunding does not carry the same type of legal restrictions because these rewards are not stock or equity. But even though it isn't as legally complex, there are still some things you should keep in mind with a crowdfunding campaign.

1. **You have to have something exciting to sell.**

   Since so many creators and entrepreneurs are using crowdfunding, you really have to have a great, fully-baked product to stand out from the crowd.

2. **Have a group of consumers who can be your evangelists.**

Again, since there are so many creators and entrepreneurs using crowdfunding, it's easy to get lost in the crowd. Having consumer evangelists who not only love your product but are willing to retweet, repost, and reblog your content will help you stand out from the crowd.

3. **Be ready to market!**

To help stand out from the crowd (Are you sensing a trend here?) you'll need to go all out on a marketing push. At the absolute bare minimum you'll need to:

- Create a short engaging video to help sell your video on your Kickstarter page.

- Have a webpage other than your Kickstarter page to help lend your venture credibility by showing more details about the current project and celebrating past successes.

- Engage with your users on social media.

- Intelligently work your press contacts and avoid sending blind press releases to journalists who don't write about products like yours.

4. **Read the terms of use and don't violate them.**

Most crowdfunding campaigns take place on private websites like Kickstarter or Indiegogo, and all of these websites have terms of service or community rules pages outlining the kind of campaigns allowed and not allowed on their sites. You'll want to read the terms carefully to ensure your carefully crafted campaign doesn't get shut down because, for instance, you violated Kickstarter's rule against offering alcohol as a reward.

5. **Have stellar rewards.**

When people contribute to your crowdfunding campaign, they are not getting any equity in your company so you'll need to offer stellar rewards to incentivize folks – besides your charming personality. In addition to offering early access to your product or your product at a discount, you'll really want to push yourself to come up with creative rewards that are relevant to your customer base. Things like writing backers into your stories, backstage passes, recording custom voicemail messages, or even offering to have an office holiday in honor of that backer and show photos of your staff celebrating, can all be great creative ways to celebrate and incentivize your backers.Keep in mind rewards based platforms aren't the only crowdfunding options. Crowdfunding is still a relatively young form of funding that is continually evolving. Here are three other types of crowdfunding that you should know about.

- Lending crowdfunding:
  Platforms like Kiva Zip allow individuals to connect with businesses that need an infusion of cash quickly. Keep in mind, as the name implies, these are loans that you'll need to pay back.

- Donation crowdfunding:
  Platforms like GoFundMe allow individuals to donate directly to businesses, people, and causes in need of funding. Donation based crowdfunding is typically best for charitable endeavors or projects that give back to the community.

- Patronage:
  Sites like Patreon allow individuals to offer a small payment every time a piece of content is released, and may even offer options to offer rewards to people who donate certain amounts. Be aware that you might not get paid unless you produce content, which could be a downside if you're just getting started on a lengthy project that won't be released for a while.

6. **Equity crowdfunding may exist.**

   The 2012 Jumpstart Our Business Startups Act (JOBS Act), was supposed to help put in place an easier way for entrepreneurs to crowdfund in return for equity instead of rewards. But it's not as easy as hopping on the non-existent equity section of your favorite crowdfunding website. First, the JOBS Act doesn't supersede state securities laws (often called "blue sky laws"). Meaning that you'll need to comply with both state and federal laws, and likely hire a lawyer to do so. Second, the final version of the JOBS Act crowdfunding rules were only recently released, so it's a bit early to say how exactly how they will play out in practice.

7. **Be prepared to act if you do get the funds.**

   You've had a successful campaign, congratulations! Now it's time to get to work creating your product and fulfilling your rewards. While setbacks and delays may happen, it's important to make sure you keep your backers updated as you work through issues.

Small Business Loans

In addition to small business loans from local banks, the US Small Business Administration[12] offers a variety of special loans just for small business owners. Many state and local small business programs offer similar loan programs. However because these government loans are designed for folks that may have been denied other loans, their interest rates can be a bit higher than normal loans. Also keep in mind government loans tend to have very specific requirements, so be sure to read them carefully before you apply.

Grants

Although grants are primarily an option for 501(c)(3) non-profits, some local and state agencies do give out small business grants. Although you don't have to pay the money back, keep in mind that grants can have stringent reporting requirements. Before investing the time to apply for a grant, be sure to do the math and make sure it won't cost you more to apply for and implement the grant than you'll be getting in grant funding.

The funding process can be a bit intimidating, but with a little bit of planning, foresight, and potentially some good legal advice, you can design the funding plan that is best for you and your endeavors.

Accelerators vs. Incubators: an early home for your project

Accelerators and incubators can provide both a home and early source of funding for your startup. While these terms are often used interchangeably, there are some important differences between them that you should know about.

Accelerators

Accelerators, as their name implies, are really intended to accelerate an existing company in a short time frame, typically ending with a chance to pitch to investors. Accelerators typically offer companies a small seed investment as well as mentorship, in return for a small amount of equity. Unlike incubators, they typically have a very competitive application process.

Incubators

Incubators are intended to incubate ideas that have not developed into a fully fleshed out company. They tend not to operate on a fixed schedule.

---

12 "SBA Loans." The U.S. Small Business Administration. Web. 23 Feb. 2016. <https://www.sba.gov/content/sba-loans>.

48

They also sometimes take more in equity than an accelerator, but not always. There are also many different types of incubators including pay to play, open invitation, or ones restricted to students at a certain university.

Incubators can also be used to describe things like IdeaLab, which are companies that come up with ideas and then find the people to staff them and build them within their incubator.

Similarities

Despite their differences both incubators and accelerators may also offer things like office space, marketing assistance, networking and presentation skill building. Also remember, it doesn't have to be an either-or decision. Some companies go through multiple incubators and accelerators during the development process.

My lawyer wants equity, what should I expect?

THE BOTTOM LINE

Attorneys may take equity in a company instead of asking for fees. However, in this type of situation, an attorney must follow very specific ethical rules to ensure they are acting in a way that will protect clients' interests and inform them of the risks.

Not following these important rules could have serious consequences for an attorney, such as losing the ownership stake in the client's company. But if your attorney isn't able to follow basic ethical rules that should be a big red flag that they might not follow the rules when it comes to preparing your documents which could cause expensive problems down the line.

Many startups can't afford attorneys to help the company navigate all of the complicated legal hurdles they will face. To deal with this problem, companies and attorneys have had to find creative ways to make business possible.

For many young businesses, this has meant giving attorneys equity instead of attorneys' fees. As you could easily imagine, this can create a conflict of interest for an attorney. How can an attorney provide neutral honest counsel when the attorney is also a part owner of a company?

49

To protect clients (as well as attorneys), most states have specific ethical rules in place that attorneys must follow when taking equity. For example, in California before an attorney can acquire ownership in a client company the attorney must first:

- Make sure the terms of the agreement are fair and reasonable.

- Fully disclose the terms of the agreement to the client.

- Explain the terms of the agreement in writing to the client in a manner that is clearly understandable.

- Advise the client in writing that the client may seek the advice of an independent lawyer of the client's choice, and give the client an opportunity to seek that advice.

- Receive consent from the client in writing to the terms of the agreement.

Keep in mind that these rules may be different where you are; but if an attorney hands you a document to sign that gives her equity in your company, without explaining it or telling you to get advice from another attorney, we recommend running away as fast as possible. You don't have to settle for an attorney who makes you uncomfortable or doesn't act ethically. Keep in mind too that there are many great law school clinics[13] and non-profits that offer free and low cost legal services to entrepreneurs and creators who won't cut ethical corners that put your company at risk.

---

13 "Law School IP and Entrepreneurship Clinics List." New Media Rights, 01 Nov. 2015. Web. 23 Feb. 2016. <http://newmediarights.org/law_school_ip_and_entrepreneurship_clinics_list>.

Chapter 7
What you Need to Know Before you Launch an Interactive Application or Internet-Based Service

Are you building a website, app, e-commerce, or other internet-based service? If so, then you know your service's features and user interface can make or break your success. Similarly, laying a solid legal foundation for your new service can also be the difference between success and failure. The good news is that there are steps you can take to protect yourself from legal liability. This chapter is all about keeping you creating and innovating, avoiding time consuming, and business ending lawsuits.

This chapter will help you protect yourself by understanding some of the key legal protections you can take advantage of when building your app or service including: terms of use, privacy policies, the Digital Millennium Copyright Act, and the Communications Decency Act, Section 230. While this chapter will provide you good overview of what you need to be thinking about, we highly recommend getting advice on your particular service from an experienced local attorney.

Terms of Use

THE BOTTOM LINE

A well-crafted terms of use should be tailored to your specific needs. Copying and pasting Facebook's terms of use onto your new e-commerce website selling various kinds of artisan kombucha will simply not do.

Your terms of use should also be made highly visible on your service. You should also require that any user or visitor that interacts with your service for anything other than basic browsing specifically agrees to your terms of use before they can interact with the service. (See below, "Why you must get users to agree to your terms and policies.") Trying to rely on a terms of use or privacy policy when users have not specifically agreed to those terms is, simply put, a bad idea.

What is a terms of use?

As internet users, many of us see the words "terms of use" and simply click "I Agree" because we want to start using the app or service, not read a lengthy contract written in legalese. But that terms of use (also known as terms of service and terms and conditions) governs the relationship between you and the users of your website, app or other internet-based service.

Why it's a good idea to have a terms of use?

As with any good relationship, setting expectations can make all the difference to solving disputes. Good terms of use will help you and your user know what to expect from each other. It's all about limiting your legal liability, making sure you have control over what content and users are allowed on your service, letting users know the limitations of your service, and encouraging desirable user behavior.

Do I even need a terms of use? Not all websites need a terms of use.
Ask yourself the following questions to figure out if you need a terms of use.

- Does your service allow users to post photos, video, or software, or integrate user content from other social media services?

- Does your service accept contact forms, email newsletter signups, or allow user comments?

- Does your service allow users to interact with the service in any other way beyond completely passive browsing?

- Does your service sell any kind of product or service?

If you said yes to any of the above questions, you should definitely be thinking about a terms of use and privacy policy. Even if you didn't say yes, if you have concerns about setting user expectations, you should be thinking about a terms of use and privacy policy.

What types of things will a good terms of use do?

While it's not exhaustive, here are some of the things a good terms of use should do for your website.

1. **Get permission to host and display user content but only get the rights you actually need.**

    If you plan to host user content on your website like images, video, data, software or blog posts you'll need to get permission from your users to host their content (known as User Generated Content or UGC) on your platform. While getting this permission is critical, you've probably seen the headlines "[Insert web service here] now owns all your content and they can do whatever they want with it!" Often this kind of sensationalist headline isn't warranted, and headlines like this are often the result of services that either tried to overreach and claim ownership over user content, or had unclear policies. When you're getting permission from your users, be sure to take only the license you need to run your service and explain to your users exactly what rights you are taking in plain language.

    CAVEAT: Always get specific consent from users for marketing campaigns.

    If your marketing efforts feature an identifiable individual or their work, it is always a good idea to get the individual's consent in addition to whatever permission you got in the terms of use. This means if you have a great photo of a few people in front of a venue having a great time and want to use the photo, or if you want to highlight a specific individual use as part of your marketing campaign, you should get explicit written consent from those users. An attorney can help you draft a document for this sort of release. Keep in mind that a user who uploads the image or likeness of other individuals can't actually give you a license to use those individuals' "likenesses" so you may need to reach out to the user to get connected with the other people in the photo. If you have any questions regarding your company's specific marketing practices now or in the future, consult an attorney.

2. **Explain to users what content will be made public.**

    If your service allows (or even encourages) sharing highly personal content and information, you need to be as clear as possible with users what information will remain public and what will remain private. As an example, if your service allows document storage, and you claim that documents stored on the service are private, there shouldn't be a technical loophole that allows the public to access those documents. We'll deal more specifically with collection of personal information in the privacy policy section below.

3. **Explain how you work with third party services.**

   Many successful services integrate with third party services these days (such as using Facebook or Google to allow users to log in). If your service integrates with third party services, you should explain to your users how the integration process works. Since you can't control third party services, it's a good idea to include language protecting your service from third party technical difficulties. Your terms can explain that you are not responsible if a user loses content or their access becomes restricted because of a third party problem. Also, you should be clear that your service may be used to share or publicly post information on third party social media sites, so the user should be careful with what information they choose to make public through the service.

4. **Tell your users what they can't do on your service.**

   In your terms of use, you should absolutely lay out what kind of behavior isn't acceptable. Maybe you're a family site and don't want users to post comments with profanity. Or maybe you've got a trove of data that you don't want people to scrape to make their own site. Bottom line, if there's behavior you're not cool with, let users know in your terms of use.

5. **Limit your liability and disclaim your warranties.**

   Most contracts (remember, terms of use are a contract) include sections on "limitations of liability" and "disclaimer of warranties". These sections are critical to limit the legal liability of your service or company, explaining to users when you are and aren't responsible for issues that arise with your service. Most terms of use also try to make sure users are the ones responsible for any illegal acts they commit using your service. This can be achieved through "indemnification" clauses, which make users responsible for any lawsuits resulting from their use your service for illegal or unauthorized activities. Realize however, that many users don't necessarily have the ability to bankroll a lawsuit, so even if your service didn't directly cause a lawsuit, you could still be on the hook to defend one.

6. **Set up a process for modifying your terms.**

   Your service will grow and change over time. You'll need the ability to modify the terms of use and privacy policy, as well as terminate the service or any part of the service at any time. You want to be clear with your users how that process for modification will work and then stick to it when the time comes. Any time you change any of your terms or policies, you must get users to affirmatively agree to the new terms for the users to be bound by them. We'll discuss how to bind users to your terms later in this chapter.

7. **Make sure you're accepted to app stores.**

Each app store has certain minimum requirements for terms of use and privacy policies which are updated on a regular basis. If you have an app, you should make sure that your terms meet these minimum requirements.

8. **Make sure you have the right to refuse service.**

No shirt, no shoes, no service. While these may not be your actual rules, it's helpful to build in the right to refuse service to any one, at any time for any reason. This clause should also be broad enough to include things like removal of content, reclaiming or denying certain user names and termination of accounts. This clause is, in essence, your trump card when a user does something unexpected and harmful on your website.

9. **Set up a process for dispute resolution.**

Good terms of use typically lay out the dispute resolution process so both parties know how disputes will be resolved. This can vary from suggesting parties try to resolve disputes informally and consider voluntary mediation, to requiring mandatory arbitration, or that all disputes be resolved in certain courts in a specific geographic location.

What is Arbitration?

Arbitration is a form of conflict resolution where parties allow an impartial third party to resolve their dispute and often serves as an alternative to litigation. Previously, mandatory binding arbitration clauses were difficult to enforce in California a court, particularly between businesses and consumers, but the law has changed relatively recently making it slightly easier. Below are some of the arguments for and against Mandatory Arbitration.

- Users are required to submit to arbitration if there is a dispute with your service or company. Some argue this allows your service and the user to avoid costly litigation and to dispose of the issue quickly and more efficiently than in court.

- The outcome of arbitration is binding, which means the appeal of a decision is rarely granted. This can save a company time because arbitration could be resolved within one year, whereas litigation can go on for many years.

- Users waive their right to a class action lawsuit, which can save your company a significant amount of money. A class action lawsuit can be costly and difficult to manage because there are so many parties involved.

- You have greater control over the time and place of the hearing. You can also choose the arbitrator (the decision maker) of your choice, which can provide you the opportunity of conducting your hearing in front of a decision maker with specialized training and credentials (instead of a layman jury).

That said, there are definitely tradeoffs and you should carefully consider whether or not you want arbitration. Below are some disadvantages to keep in mind:

- Arbitration is estimated to cost an average of $10,000 total for an entire arbitration proceeding.

- Although binding arbitration may save you time and money, since the decision is final, this also means you will be bound if the outcome is unfavorable.

- From a public relations standpoint, consumers often view mandatory binding arbitration clauses as unfair to the consumer, and you may not think it's worth it to fight a public relations battle.

Ultimately, whether or not you decide to include an arbitration clause in your terms of use is your decision, and if you have further questions regarding this issue, or another mode of conflict resolution that you had in mind, you should carefully discuss it with your attorney.

Privacy Policies

Privacy policies are detailed disclosures of the information that is being collected by your service and how that information is used.

When companies don't provide this kind of information clearly to users in their privacy policy, privacy lawsuits and FTC investigations are a very real possibility. In some states, such as California, certain types of services that collect personal identifying information from users are **required** to have readily available privacy policies.

If you're collecting any sort of personal information or data from users, such as name, address, email, credit card information, location, or device ID, you'll want to have a privacy policy.

When making a detailed disclosure, be sure to be very clear about how you will use user data and personal information. The more that services hide in these disclosures, the more likely it is that successful privacy-related lawsuits can occur. This is something all services and companies want to avoid.

A good privacy policy will both protect your service and provide users with notice of how their information is used. Specifically, a good privacy policy should address the following:

1. **The information you collect and how you use it.**

    Let the user know what type of information is collected by the service; what kind of control they have over what information is collected by the service; and place limits on how they may use the service.

2. **Information users provide to you.**

    A good privacy policy should address the information that users provide to the service themselves, including contact and billing information for purposes of making purchases on the website.

3. **Information learned from the user's mobile device.**

If your service can be used on a mobile device, your privacy policy should include a section that focuses on telling the user what type of information is collected for the service when used on a mobile device. Information gathered from a mobile device may include things like location, time, and device ID number.

4. **How you share user information with others.**

Don't forget about those third parties! Let your users know in the privacy policy whether and how their personal information is being shared with third-party services. Even if you don't plan on sharing user information with third parties, it's a good idea to let users know you have the right to do so. There are certain instances when you likely will share information with third parties, like if the user gives consent, if you are legally required to do so, or if it's otherwise necessary to enforce your terms or policies. If you don't do this, you could find yourself in a catch-22, either breaking your word to users, or saying no to a judge who has ordered your service to release information.

5. **How users can remove their information.**

Let users know when they can contact you for removal of personal information from your service.

6. **The process for modifying your privacy policy.**

Your service will grow and change. As we've mentioned, you'll need the ability to modify the terms of use and privacy policy. You want to be clear with your users how that process for modification will work and then stick to it when the time comes.

If your privacy policy accurately addresses each of the points above, you know you're headed in the right direction. That said, many states have specific laws about what must go in your privacy policy, so be sure to check in with an attorney in your state to make sure your privacy policy is compliant.

Other Policies, Including Community Guidelines, Return Policies, Product Disclaimers, and More

THE BOTTOM LINE

Beyond terms of use and privacy policies, there are other kinds of policies and contracts that you may want to have your users agree to when they interact with your service. A highly interactive service should have community guidelines, and one that sells products should consider a product disclaimer and return policy.

Community Guidelines

If you are running a site based on heavy community participation, community guidelines are absolutely necessary. These human readable guidelines are a great place to let users know types of behavior are encouraged (such as respecting others and having fun), and which are unacceptable (such as cyberbullying or spam). It's also a good place to let users know how to contact you with requests to remove material that they find offensive or inappropriate. By putting users on notice of what is acceptable on your platform and how to report problems, these guidelines can help you minimize negative behavior and help you establish the type of community you're seeking to establish.

Return Policies

For businesses selling physical products, having a return policy that is clear and legally sound is critical (and is a legal requirement in some states). The return policy generally sets customer expectations about how and when an item can be returned. A good return policy often addresses the following:

- How soon a customer needs to contact you after receiving the product to request a return.

- Whether certain items marked as "Final Sale" or "As Is" can be returned.

- Make sure to actually follow your policy and mark items correctly if they are not available for return.

- What condition items must be in to be returned.

- What else must be included with a returned item, such as a copy of the receipt.

- Whether there is a restocking fee. If so, when does it apply?

- Whether returns are available as refunds, store credit, and/or exchanges.

- Any other requirements or information necessary to clarify your return policy

Remember, a return policy won't do you much good if your users don't know it exists. Consider placing it in several prominent areas of your website and consider having users agree to it as part of the check out process.

Product Disclaimers

Terms of use apply to the actual use of your internet based app or service. A product disclaimer, however, addresses the actual products that you sell, and attempts to limit your liability. Again, a product disclaimer is most relevant when you're selling physical products. Product disclaimers state that you are not liable for any improper or dangerous uses, modifications, or abuse of the products, typically disclaiming liability to the extent permitted by law. Product disclaimers also often explain that you may change any of the product descriptions, images and specifications of products.

Other types of policies

Each app or service has unique features, and you'll want to carefully consider (ideally with your lawyer) what other types of policies you may need. Is your new service some kind of subscription service? Do you have some sort of affiliate program? You'll want to lay the details of those policies out to your users.

THE BOTTOM LINE

Terms of use, privacy policies, or any other contract you want users to agree to are useless if users haven't actually agreed to them.

Users must accept your terms and policies prior to registering as a user or interacting with your service (on both the web service and the mobile application). This means users shouldn't be able to post any content of any kind on the service, make a purchase, make a comment, or submit any forms without agreeing to the relevant terms and policies.

This is typically done by providing a required check box that says something like "by clicking this box, I affirm I have read and am bound by the terms of use (link) and privacy policy (link) [and any other relevant policies] of this service." This box and attached links to the TOU and privacy policy should be above the "submit and agree button." This provides clear evidence that the user was exposed to all three documents, and decreases the likelihood of success against any claim that the user never consented to or wasn't aware of such documents.

Where else should you post your terms of use, privacy policy, and other policies?

Links to your terms and policies should be posted in a conspicuous, easy to find place on your service. Many services place these links at the bottom of the service or app login/profile page, although there is a growing preference that these links be placed at the top of the page so they are even more conspicuous. The general rule is that the more clearly and conspicuously they're posted, the clearer it is that users are bound by the terms and policies.

Create and maintain internal links within your policies

When posting the terms of use and privacy policy on your company's website, consider adding "anchor links" to sections of your terms of use.

Anchor links, like those found in Wikipedia articles, function as a table of contents and greatly increase readability and ultimately, enforceability.

How to Protect Your Service from Copyright Infringement by Your Users: The Digital Millennium Copyright Act Safe Harbors

The Digital Millennium Copyright Act Safe Harbors

Before the Digital Millennium Copyright Act (DMCA) was passed any website that wanted to host user generated digital content faced substantial liability under a copyright system that simply wasn't equipped to deal with the digital age. So in 1998 Congress passed the DMCA, in part to create a structure that tried to provide more legal certainty for websites that hosted user generated content. In this section we'll explain who qualifies for these Safe Harbors and how to comply with the Safe Harbors.

It takes affirmative steps to get DMCA Safe Harbor protection

To protect your service from liability for users' copyright infringement, the DMCA provides a series of safe harbors you'll want to know about. However, there are steps you must actively complete in order to get and keep DMCA safe harbor protection. Let's look at how you qualify for, obtain, and maintain DMCA protection.

THE BOTTOM LINE

If your service is based online and you're allowing others to post content on or through your service, you are probably a service provider. Always remember that nothing in the DMCA Safe Harbors protects material you or your employees post on the service beyond some limited protection for linking to other websites. The safe harbors are intended as protections from user copyright infringement for services that simply provide a place for sharing and communication among end users.

If you want to use the DMCA safe harbor, you have to be a "service provider." The good news is that the definition of service provider is quite broad and covers many different services that host or link to content. If you do any of the following, you'll probably be a service provider.

1. **Acting as a pipeline for internet traffic**

    This safe harbor is typically used by internet access providers, like Comcast or AT&T, to shield their activities because the providers simply act as a "pipe" for internet traffic.

2. **Caching activities**

    This safe harbor was originally intended to cover servers automatically storing information in order to improve internet speed and performance. It covers automated intermediate and temporary storage of information. It's a narrow class of services that are less common now than they were in 1998, but if you are providing internet service and you need to store copies of things to speed up your service, you may be covered.

3. **Content and information stored on a service**

    This safe harbor covers information that a user stores on a network or system. This covers everyone from social media websites to cloud storage providers. We'll focus in quite a bit on this category since many companies fall into this bucket.

4. Acting as a search engine or providing links

This safe harbor covers search engines and services that refer or link users to other online locations through directories, indexes, and hyperlinks.

The key safe harbor that protects interactive services, Section 51

THE BOTTOM LINE

If you're hosting content that users upload, you need to do everything in this section to get protection from the DMCA. But remember that the safe harbor does not protect content that you, your service, or your employees post.

What you have to do to get protection under the DMCA Section 512(c) Safe Harbor: Basic Requirements.

To qualify for the §512(c) safe harbor, a service provider must take several affirmative steps and establish specific business practices. First of all, as we discussed above, you need to qualify as a "service provider," which includes a very broad variety of apps and internet services. Here are the other requirements you must meet to get protection under the DMCA:

1. Register your site and designate a DMCA Agent with the Copyright Office.

To get DMCA protection you'll have to have a copyright agent. This is the person at your company (or an outside provider you hire) that will receive and process all DMCA notifications. To register your agent you'll need to go to http://www.copyright.gov/onlinesp/ to print out the form and send in a snail mail version of the form along with a fee of $105. When you register it's a good idea to pick a person that will be around for a while because you need to keep your agent information up to date and you'll need to pay the $105 fee every time you update their information.

2. **Your service should post the contact information for your DMCA agent on your website or app.**

   This is typically done in the terms of use and wherever copyright complaints are submitted.

3. **Adopt a policy that your service will terminate repeat infringers and reasonably implement it.**

   Typically this means terminating users after a set amount of copyright infringement claims. A common standard is 3 strikes, though users should be given the opportunity to counternotice (discussed below), and if they do so, the strike should not count against them. It's also a good idea to provide specific procedures for copyright owners to rescind takedown notices in case they mistakenly send a takedown notice. When writing out your official policy you must include the following sentence, "provide for the termination in appropriate circumstances of subscribers and account holders of the service provider's system or network who are repeat infringers." While your service may choose to adopt and provide more detailed information on your procedures, your service is only required to include the language in the previous sentence.

4. **Communicate your policy for takedowns, counternotices, the termination of repeat infringers and your overall copyright policy to the users of your website.**

   This information should be included in your terms of use and ideally on a separate page that just addresses your copyright policies. Make sure both pages are easy to find on your website.

5. **Accommodate and not interfere with "standard technical measures" used by copyright owners to identify or protect copyrighted works.**

   This requirement is not as clear since there are not really standard technical measures that exist. However, you should avoid taking steps solely designed to interfere with copyright owners identifying their content on your service.

THE BOTTOM LINE

Besides the basic requirements for DMCA protection, you also need to make sure your service is acting swiftly to respond to takedown notices, and that you've consulted with a lawyer to make sure you're avoiding the kind of marketing and business model choices that could make you lose your DMCA protection.

You're probably thinking, "That can't be all the requirements for DMCA protection, could it?" If so you're right, there's more, but stick with us and it'll all be worth it. In addition to registering an agent, and adopting and implementing a policy to terminate repeat infringers, the DMCA lays out additional requirements to meet in order to be protected by the safe harbor. Essentially, your service cannot have knowledge of specific copyright infringement or engage in any behavior that encourages copyright infringement through your service. If your service is primarily focused on activities that have nothing to do with copyright infringement, then you are headed in the right direction. Specifically, a service provider should build business practices that ensure the service:

1. **Lack actual knowledge of the infringement.**

   This means you can't know that people are actively uploading specific illegal content onto your service. This type of actual knowledge is especially problematic when the company's own employees upload illegal content, particularly if they are instructed to do so by management.

2. **Or lack awareness of facts and circumstances from which infringement might be apparent.**

   Sometimes known as "red flag knowledge" this is a subjective test that looks at whether a reasonable person would have been aware of specific instances of infringement based on the available facts. So while knowing that infringement may exist on your platform generally isn't enough, if information has been provided to your team that may be enough for red flag knowledge. If this standard seems a bit fuzzy, that's because it is. Courts have really struggled to define this standard in a coherent way.

3. **If you have either type of knowledge listed above, you must act expeditiously to remove or disable access to, the infringing material.**

    This means when you get a valid DMCA takedown notice you need to act on it very quickly. How quickly? At the time of writing there is a case pending about whether a takedown 48 hours after receiving a notice was too long.[14] While it's unclear how that case will turn out, removing content as quickly as possible is important.

4. **If you have the right and ability to control the infringement, you can't have a financial interest in the infringement.**

    Again, this is a standard that courts have really struggled to define and practically apply. Here courts usually look for services that are directly profiting from copyright infringement, and the services that avoid this are often to show that their pricing structures and business model was neutral towards all users, rather than specifically profiting from infringement. Because of the particular uncertainty of this factor, it may be a good idea to talk through your service's features with a lawyer to see if this could be a problem for your site.

    Despite the requirements we've discussed, your service is not required to actively seek out infringing content and is not permitted to violate users' privacy rights in gaining access to potentially infringing content.

How to handle DMCA Takedown notices as a service provider

THE BOTTOM LINE

You've got a number of requirements you must meet to gain DMCA safe harbor protection. To keep it, you need to respond swiftly to takedown notices and counternotices. Learn how the takedown and counternotice process works, and what your service needs to do when it receives a takedown or counternotice, by reading below.

---

14   Square Ring, Inc. v. UStream.com. District Court of Delaware.

The DMCA contains specific requirements for takedown notices. Takedown notices are notifications by a copyright owner to a service provider that claim copyright infringement by a user and request that the service provider take down the infringing material. As a service provider, you don't have to respond to takedown notices that don't meet the requirements below.

What should be in a Takedown Notice

An effective takedown notice must be in writing, must be directed to the service provider's designated agent (discussed above), and must contain the following:

- A physical or electronic signature of the person authorized to act on behalf of the copyright owner;

- Identification of the copyrighted work that is the object of the claimed infringement;

- Identification of the material claimed to be infringing and information reasonably sufficient to enable the service provider to locate the material;

- Contact information for the party complaining of the infringement;

- A statement that the party complaining has "a good faith belief that the use of the material in question is not authorized by the copyright owner, its agent, or the law"; and

- A statement, under penalty of perjury, that the complaining party is authorized to act for the copyright owner and that the information in the notification is accurate.

A takedown notice must be from the actual copyright owner.

Only the copyright owner or an authorized agent can send a DMCA takedown notice. People who are not copyright owners or authorized agents (like a lawyer or rights enforcement company) of a copyright owner might occasionally send you a takedown notice — but any such notices have no legal effect and your service doesn't need to act on bogus notices.

What to do when you've received a valid takedown notice.

If you receive a valid takedown notice that meets the requirements described above, your service must act "expeditiously" to remove or disable access to the allegedly infringing content. You'll also need to take reasonable steps to promptly notify the user who posted the content that the content has been removed. The user then has an opportunity to send a counternotice.

Contents of the Counter-Notification.

If a user believes that his or her material was wrongly taken down, the user may send a counternotice to the service provider's DMCA agent. The counternotice must include:

- A signature (electronic or physical) of the user identification of the material that was removed or disabled and the location at which it appeared before removal.

- A statement, under penalty of perjury, that "the user has a good faith belief that the material was removed or disabled as a result of mistake or misidentification of the material."

- The user's name, address, and telephone number, and a statement that the user consents to federal court jurisdiction and accepts service of process from the person who provided the original notification.

As noted above, the service provider will provide the copyright owner (or its agent) with a copy of the counternotice, and the copyright owner may then file suit against the user.

What to do when you've received a valid counternotice?

If you receive a valid counternotice, you must promptly send the person who sent the original takedown notice a copy of the counternotice, and inform that person that you will repost the content or re-enable access in 10 business days. You then must re-enable access or repost the content in 10-14 business days after receipt of the counternotice, unless you receive notice that the copyright owner has filed a lawsuit against the alleged infringer.

THE BOTTOM LINE

CDA §230 protects your service from all sorts of legal liability that could come from user activity, with a few key exceptions like intellectual property and federal criminal laws. As long as you're not actively encouraging users to do illegal things, you should be able to get §230 protection.

The DMCA safe harbor, discussed above, was all about protecting your service from copyright infringement. CDA §230 protects you and your service from a wide variety of other kinds of legal liability. Unlike the DMCA safe harbors, you don't need to take affirmative steps to get protection through CDA §230. There are no requirements to file information with a government agency, adopt policies to terminate services to repeat violators, and no notice and takedown procedures. If you qualify, you simply aren't responsible for most unlawful content posted by a third party.

The basics

CDA §230 protects those who create apps and internet based services from liability for content and statements someone else who is not an employee put on your service. It can also protect you if someone is using your service for illegal activity. It is hard to overstate how important this immunity is to online services.

Is the CDA §230 really that different from traditional publisher liability?

Yes. It's important to recognize that CDA §230 is very different from liability for the statements of others offline in media like newspapers and magazines. Traditionally, in cases dealing with liability for defamatory or unlawful content in print media, both the author of the content and the publisher (due to its editorial control over the content) would be held liable. However, the distributor (such as a newsstand or bookstore) would not be liable. These concepts were difficult to apply in the context of the internet, so Congress enacted §230 to protect the middle man on the internet.

70

Which Online Activities Are Protected by §230?

What CDA §230 doesn't cover

Section 230 is often used to defend against claims of defamation or invasion of privacy and has been used to immunize apps and services from a wide variety of state and federal lawsuits. The immunity is broad, but it's not universal. The few exceptions that it does not cover include intellectual property claims (copyright, trademark, and patent), federal criminal law, and claims brought under the Electronic Communications Privacy Act (used to prosecute a wide variety of computer related crimes).

Activities covered by §230

Section 230 immunity is usually available if you don't alter the meaning of the original content. This immunity has been applied broadly to the activities of apps and internet-based services.

The following activities are typically protected by CDA §230:

1. **Screening content before publication**

   You can screen content before it's posted on your service and still be protected. Screening content before publication is exactly the kind of activity that §230 was specifically designed to immunize.

2. **Selecting content for publication**

   Your service can select specific content for publication from a pool of user-submitted material without losing §230 immunity.

3. **Correcting, editing, or removing content**

   Your service can perform some editorial functions, including correcting, editing, and removing content, and still be protected by CDA §230. But you can't make extensive editorial changes that alter the meaning of the user-generated content like making a non-defamatory statement defamatory.

4. **Paying a third party to create or submit content.**

   As long as the author is not an employee of your service, you will not lose §230 immunity if you pay a third party for the content.

5. **Encouraging users to submit content.**

   Successful apps and services' ability to survive and thrive is often dependent on hosting and republishing user-generated content. Soliciting and encouraging users to participate in a social media service by submitting content does not remove protection under §230. The one caveat to this is that your service should actively avoid directly encouraging or facilitating any illegal behavior or content submissions by your users.

6. **Providing forms or drop-down menus to allow users to submit content.**

   Providing forms that allow your users to submit content has been protected as long as the forms are neutral and don't encourage users to break the law. But how could someone break the law with a drop down menu? For example let's say you ran a website that helped people find roommates and you had a series of dropdown menus that let users specify the gender, race and religion of their ideal roommate. Under federal law advertisements for housing can't have this type of information so by providing these menus you're helping your users break federal law.

7. **Leaving content up after the site has been notified that material is defamatory.**

   Section 230 provides immunity even if an interactive computer service is informed of alleged defamatory material and chooses to leave the content up. Some services have ethical or business considerations that compel them to remove certain user-generated content, but unlike under the DMCA, §230 immunity does not disappear merely because the service provider fails or refuses to remove the content.

   There was a lot of information in this chapter! While this chapter is a great way to get yourself up to speed, if you're running an interactive website or app it would be a really good idea to at least have a conversation with an attorney about some of the things in this chapter to make sure you're on the right track.

Part II
Creating, Licensing, and Distributing Content

Chapter 8
How to License Anything and When to get Permission

When you want to use something that someone else created in your own work, there are all kinds of rights to think about. Is what you want to use protected by copyright, patent, trademark, rights of publicity, or various rights to privacy? (See Chapter 2) If your use isn't otherwise allowed by the law, such as through fair use, the public domain, or an open license, you probably need written permission. In this chapter, we're going to help you start to understand when to get written permission, and the kinds of permission you may need to move your project forward.

What is a license?

A license is simply written permission that you can reuse something. Permission can vary from a broad license that allows you to do nearly anything you want, to a very narrow, tailored license that only allows a very particular use.

You may need permission to make a script into a film, use software for your business, or utilize another's patented invention as part your new invention.

A license is not ownership

Remember that a license is not ownership. To transfer ownership you usually need what's called an assignment. The only exception is that in some cases, when you're working with a contractor that's creating copyrighted work for you, you can contract with them to create a "work for hire." "Work for hire" is only available in specific circumstances, and means you automatically own the copyright to the work the contractor creates under the contract, requiring no assignment of rights later on.

I've been told I can reuse this, and I trust the people I'm working with, so why do I need anything in writing?

While trust is the foundation of any good relationship, it's also important that the promises and expectations in that relationship be clear. Parties who trust each other can still disagree about what was said, and while email is easy to write, it can easily create misunderstandings. When many emails have gone back and forth, the "agreement" can become unclear, and it's easy for even friendly parties to disagree about who made what promises.

The only way to make solid promises and set clear expectations that are enforceable is to have a written agreement (preferably written by an attorney) that both parties sign. In fact, the best written agreements can help save you time and money, giving both parties a document they can look back to for clarification. This helps avoid disputes, keeping you moving your project forward.

Written agreements don't have to be overwhelmingly long documents full of only legalese either. If your lawyer is creating these kinds of convoluted contracts for you, they should explain why that's necessary, or you may consider getting a new lawyer who can help build you contracts that better fit your business.

Common licenses you might need

Just as human creativity is almost infinite, so are the types of agreements to help license that creativity. Below we'll discuss some common licenses.

Writer Agreements

You may be hiring someone to write a series of scripts, blogs, news articles, or other written work for you. In many cases, you may have that writer transfer ownership to you through an assignment agreement. However, if you're not transferring ownership, make sure to be thorough about describing how you are going to use their writing in the license.

Are you only allowed to use the article on the web, or also in a book you're writing? Are you just allowed to use the script for this one film, or can you create your own adaptations of the script for a web series or sequel?

Materials Releases

A materials release allows you to use a photo, video, or other copyrighted work in your project. These are most commonly used for video creators. In a materials release, you want to be thorough about describing how you are going to reuse the works. For instance, if you get permission to use a photo only in a YouTube video, but then adapt that video into a longer film that screens at film festivals and on broadcast stations, you probably don't have the correct license to use that photo in the film.

User-Generated Content license for an internet based app or service

This license is usually included in the terms of use. As discussed in our terms of use section, an internet based app or service that allows users to share and display copyrighted content with others should get a license from its users to share and display that content. It's important to get the rights you need to make your service function, without vastly overreaching and creating a PR nightmare for your fledgling service.

Software licenses

If you didn't create the software, you probably need a license to use it. A software license typically tells you exactly how you can use the software, whether for personal or business use, and for how many users. If you're using licensed software in your business, make sure you're following the license. If you're working with contract developers to create software code that you plan to use in your own software, you probably want to own that code through an assignment agreement.

API licenses

Application Programming Interfaces (APIs) allow you to integrate with other software and use data and content from other services. If your new app or service uses an API to utilize data and content from another service, you'll want to make sure you're within the bounds of the API license. Just because the API gives you access to certain data or content, doesn't mean you can use it for any purpose.

What are the consequences if I don't follow an API?

As with many licenses, if you don't follow an API license, it can result in anything from a nasty letter from a lawyer to litigation. If your app or service relies on other services to function, losing access to that service could mean the end of your service.

Here's what you should be thinking about when you want to use APIs.

1. **Avoid being a direct competitor**

    Most services that offer API licenses are trying to encourage use of the service without empowering direct competitors. For example, integrating and displaying Yelp reviews for your company on your company's website is fine (as long as you follow all the requirements in the API), but using Yelp data to create a service that directly competes against Yelp is not.

2. **Use the API, don't scrape content**

    Content scraping is when you take content from one website or service and use it or publish it on your own website or service. Most terms of use restrict scraping, so using the API is generally a better way to avoid violating the terms of use.

3. **Attribution is often important**

    Attribution is often written into the API license agreements and policies, and there's no way to get a service upset faster than using their content but not offering folks a way to plug-in to that original service quickly.

Patent license

If you're interested in using someone's patented invention, you should make sure to get permission to use that invention.

Trademark licenses

Remember that trademark law is all about preventing consumer confusion. If you want to use a trademark of another company, on your product or service, you probably need permission. For example, if you want to incorporate a sports team's logo on products you're selling on your e-commerce website, you probably need permission.

The main difference between an open licenses and traditional licenses is that open licenses typically allow the public to reuse something without negotiating for direct written permission. There are all kinds of open licenses, and they can be attached to everything from software to photos, music, and videos.
As long as you reuse the work within the terms of the license, you should be good to go. If you want to use the work for something not permitted in the open license, you'll need to negotiate for written permission. We'll cover this type of licensing more in the next chapter.

Music Licensing

Music is awesome, but from a licensing standpoint it can be very confusing. So we've created a special section just to talk about music licensing.

How to ask for a license

Now that you know you need a license how do you get one? Here are 5 things you should do when asking for a license.

1. **Think about how you want to use the work before contacting a representative**

   To make the licensing process go smoothly, you should be prepared to clearly articulate to the owner exactly how you want to use the content before talking to a representative. If you come in prepared and clear with your licensing request, you're likely to get a quicker response and a better license.

2. **Identify the owner**

   The next thing you should do is search for some basic information about whatever it is you want to reuse. Specifically, figure out who owns the copyright, patent, trademark, or other rights you need. This may not be entirely clear until you reach out and ask for permission, but start by identifying the individual or company that created or invented what you want to use.

3. **Be specific and clear**

   When you contact a licensing representative and negotiate for a license, be as specific as possible. You want to make sure you obtain the rights and permissions that you need. You might need multiple different types of licenses, so clarity and precision is key. And be persistent, the costs of licenses vary, but you may be able to negotiate for a reduced rate.

4. **Make sure you got the actual rights you need**

   Once you've actually been issued a license, make sure the specific written license doesn't leave out important rights you'll need.

5. **Always read the license**

   Regardless of what is said in negotiations, make sure that you understand whatever you sign before you sign it. Beware of parties that want you to sign on the dotted line without reading anything!

Things you should almost always get assigned.

THE BOTTOM LINE

Any contractors or volunteers that aren't your employees own what they're creating. This means you need to get an agreement from them "assigning" (transferring) the rights to what they're contributing if you want to clearly own what you're creating.

Here are the kinds of situations where an assignment (transfer) of any rights is more common than a license.

Creative materials like logos, artwork, photos, website designs, and advertisements.

Certain artwork or photos might be central to the look and feel you're trying to create. If you're working with an independent contractor or volunteer artist to create a logo or other artwork for you, you should make sure to get that logo and artwork assigned. The same goes for contract photographers and video creators. If you're trying to maintain a unique look and feel, an assignment will make sure that (1) the creative material doesn't start appearing in other works, and (2) you actually have the ability to pursue copyright infringements as the copyright owner.

Interviewee, Actor, Director, and Crew Releases

These are typically written permission from interviewees, actors, directors, and crewmembers that are working on a film or video that says you have the right to any copyrighted expression they may have created for the project. The idea is that any creative work they contribute to the film will be owned by you. Getting these rights assigned is important when you try to distribute your film or video, because distributors typically want to know that you have all the rights to whatever you're trying to distribute. In addition, an assignment makes sure (1) your crew or director doesn't repurpose your creative material and (2) that you can pursue copyright infringement as the copyright owner.

Software code

As mentioned, if you're working with contract developers to create software code you plan to use in your own software, you probably want to own that code through an assignment. Without it, you could see your code show up in places you didn't expect, such as a competitor's product.

Music Licensing —
Breaking it Down: Things to Think About When You Want to Use Music.

Music can be a powerful creative tool for video creators, podcasters, game developers, and many other creators. That said, music is one of the most difficult types of creative works to license. The reason it's so challenging is that there are multiple layers of rights to consider for each song: the rights to the composition (typically the sheet music and lyrics), the rights to the recording of a song, the performance rights, rights to any arrangements, rights to record a new sound recording, and rights to synchronize a sound recording with video, just to name a few. Here's a breakdown of some of the basics for getting permission to use music.

"Song" = Musical Composition + Sound Recording

It is important to understand that a recorded song itself has two parts: the musical composition and the sound recording. The musical composition is made up of the written lyrics and the musical notes – it's the original sheet music. The sound recording is the recording artist's specific recorded version of the song, whether recorded as a solo track or with a band. Copyright law protects each half of this musical equation separately because each is a different creative step, often produced by different people. Once you realize that copyright in most music is split between the composition and sound recording, and that each of those copyrighted works has its own bundle of rights attached to it (restricting copying, distribution, performance, derivatives etc – see our discussion of copyright law in Chapter 3), you can see how music licensing questions get complicated quickly.

Unless you have a reason you're allowed to use the music under fair use (which is rare as we explain in Chapter 10), you should always try to obtain permission from the correct copyright owner. Just be aware that you may have to track down multiple copyright owners and performance rights organizations to fully clear the music you want to use.

Don't Forget About the Arrangement!

An arrangement is a re-conceptualization of an existing musical composition. It often involves adding to the original work or reconstructing the harmonies and melodies. Many times arrangements change or add to the original composition so much that the new arrangement has its own copyright protection as a derivative (adaptation) of the original. It is important to keep track of both the composition and the arrangement. This is especially true if you want to use a song that you think is in the public domain, because while an original musical composition may be in the public domain, a later arrangement of that composition might not be. For example, the original musical composition to the popular folk song Amazing Grace might be in the public domain and freely available to use, but the particular arrangement that you've found might not be. If that arrangement has its own copyright protection, you need permission from the owner of the arrangement, and if it's not an original recording of the song that you've already licensed, you would likely need the rights to the song recording as well.

Who Owns What?

The copyright owner of a particular musical composition or sound recording is not always simply the person who created it. Copyright owners of the composition are often the songwriter or the music publisher, or sometimes a combination of both. The copyright owner of the song recording is sometimes the recording artist, but the recording artist might also assign (transfer) their copyrights (in whole or in part) to a record label. Remember that permission to use a song must come from both:

- The copyright owner of the composition (or the arrangement) and,

- The copyright owner of the sound recording.

Remember, even though you may have bought a song from a music store like Amazon, you only have the rights to listen to the music – you do not own the rights to use that song in a film, and must still obtain permission from the copyright owner to use the song.

Types of Music Licenses

Licenses give legal permission to use another's music in certain ways. There are different licenses depending on how you would like to use the music.

1. **Master Use License**

   This license applies to the sound recording, giving you the legal right to reproduce the sound recording in your project. "Master" refers to the master recording of the song, and includes all of the sounds present in the recording. Contact the owner of the sound recording for this license (usually the record label).

2. **Synchronization License**

   This license allows you to use a musicalcomposition in "sync" with visual content in audio-visual works (films, videos, websites and television) that will later be exhibited in movie theaters, on television, online or in other public forums. Whenever you want to synchronize music with visual content, this is the license you will need (along with the master use license). Typically you contact the owner of the composition for a sync license (usually the music publisher). Another specific source is Songfreedom, which has a fairly large music database to choose from, and it offers sync licenses as well as other commercial use licenses.

3. **Compulsory Licenses—Generally**

   Compulsory means the copyright owner can't say no to you. They must give you a license as long as you pay the proper royalties. In addition to the public performance and "mechanical" licenses for cover songs (discussed below), there are a number of additional compulsory licenses in copyright law, including everything from jukeboxes to subscription and non-subscription digital audio transmission (like internet radio). Navigating compulsory licenses can get difficult quickly, so we highly recommend talking to an experienced music attorney to navigate the licenses you need. Make sure to check whether the compulsory license you want to use requires you to file a notice of intention to obtain a compulsory license with the Copyright Office, and make sure to pay any royalties owed to the copyright owner.

4. **Compulsory Licenses—Public Performance License**

This compulsory license is required whenever a composition is broadcast on the radio, television, in live venues, and public places. This might be a license to consider if you intend on staging and later filming a performance of that musical composition. These licenses are available through performance rights organizations such as Broadcast Music, Inc. (BMI), the American Society of Composers, Authors and Publishers (ASCAP), and SESAC, Inc. Also note that if the performance of the song is a focal point in your film, you will need permission (preferably in writing) from the performers in order to use their performances in your film (we'll explain why in Chapter 13).

5. **Compulsory Licenses—Mechanical License:**

The key license for cover songs. This is an important subset of the compulsory licenses. This is the license you will need if you want record your own, new version of a song. The mechanical license allows you to reproduce and distribute original sound recordings of an existing musical composition in physical or digital form. The nice part about this license is that the copyright owner <u>must</u> give you a license as long as:

- You pay the proper royalties;

- The composition is non-dramatic
  (meaning it's not an opera or a musical);

- The composition has already been recorded. If the composition had not been previously recorded, manufactured and distributed, the mechanical license will have to be negotiated for from the original copyright owner directly;

- The previous recording must have been distributed publicly in the U.S. and;

- It will be used for audio purposes only (this does not cover use the recording with video).

To purchase a mechanical license, check out Harry Fox Agency, Loudr, and Easy Song Licensing. So if you want to release your own sound recording of a song on Amazon, iTunes, SoundCloud, or elsewhere, the Mechanical license is probably what you need. Remember, however, that even if you've created a cover recording, to use this new sound recording as part of a video, you will still need to get a synchronization license as described above.

How Do I Navigate This Mess? How to Ask For Music Licenses

Some of these steps are similar to our general how to ask for licenses guide, but we've added some specific nuances for music below.

1. **Think about purpose, exhibition and distribution before contacting a representative**

    » Think about how you want to use the song – Will you be using it as:

    - Background music in a video, podcast, or video game?

    - In the opening or closing credits?

    - The focal point of a scene?

    - How many times will you use the song, and for how long?

    » Then think about how your project will reach your intended audience:

    - If it's a video project, are you making this video for a school project?

    - Do you intend to submit it to a film festival?

    - Plan to screen it in a movie theater (known as theatrical rights)?

    - In DVD format?

    - Video on demand, or strictly online streaming?

    - Will your video, podcast, or game be available in other countries?

Thinking about how you want to use the song within your creative work, and how the audience will access your work will be very helpful in figuring out the type of license you will need. To make the process go smoothly, you need to be prepared to clearly articulate exactly what rights you need before talking to a representative. These representatives are used to making deals with other licensing professionals daily, and if you come in prepared and clear you're likely to get a quicker response and a better license.

2. **Do a basic search, and identify the copyright owner.**

   If or when you find a particular song to use within your video, podcast, or video game, the next thing you should do is search for some basic information about the song. Specifically, take note of who owns the copyright (the record label who produced the song and the publishing house), and the date the song was published. If a musician you're working with wants to make their own original sound recording of a musical composition, ask the musician for a copy of the sheet music. This will help you figure out who the copyright owners of the composition are.

3. **Be specific and clear.**

   When you contact a licensing representative and negotiate for a license, be as specific as possible. You want to make sure you obtain the rights and permissions that you need. You might need multiple different types of licenses, so clarity and precision are key. And be persistent, the costs of licenses vary, but you can negotiate for a reduced rate.

4. **Make sure you got the actual rights you need.**

   Once you've actually been issued a license, make sure the specific written license doesn't leave out important rights you'll need.

Keep calm, be persistent, and keep creating!

It may seem daunting when you think about the tangled web of music rights, but don't get discouraged!

Finding the copyright owner or the rights organization that controls the appropriate rights is sometimes a difficult task, and will require some digging. If you are having a hard time finding the true copyright owner, consider reaching out to a music rights attorney.

Fair Use & Music.

If you're just using a song simply because you like the way it sounds, and you think your viewers and listeners will like the way it sounds, that's typically not enough to use the song without permission under fair use. Music tends to be one of the hardest areas to make a fair use argument. However, there are certain circumstances where your use of another's song might be considered fair use, including parody or instances where you're directly criticizing a portion of a song. To learn more about fair use, check out our chapter on fair use.

Creative Commons, Open Licensing, and Music.

Also remember that open licensed music is always an option for your project – check out our guide[15] to finding openly licensed content.

A good rule of thumb is to stop and think, do I use music in anything I'm doing? Everything from apps to yoga studios to restaurants use music. If you're using music in any way, ask yourself: do I have permission to use this, or is there any other reason that I'm allowed to use this? If the answer is no, it's time to figure out what music licenses you may need.

---

15 "How to Find Free Music, Images, and Video You Can Use or Remix in Your Own Creative Works." New Media Rights, 18 Feb. 2009. Web. 23 Feb. 2016. <http://www.newmediarights.org/guide/how_to/social_media/social_video/find_free_music_images_video_use_remix_creative_works>.

Chapter 9
How Open Licensing can Benefit you!

THE BOTTOM LINE

If you're looking to encourage collaboration, sharing, and remixing, open licenses like Creative Commons and GPL might be for you.

Open licenses, like the Creative Commons (CC) license suite and the GNU Public License (GPL), allow content creators and software developers to license their work in ways that allow the public to share and use a creative work – under certain conditions.

By default, copyright law says that when you as a creator or software developer create, that expression is automatically copyrighted and you can control how the work is used. So why would you ever consider open licensing your work? Lots of reasons, including that "all rights reserved" can be an overly restrictive, one-size-fits-all application for certain creators and developers. If your mission is to seek to encourage collaboration, sharing and remixing, open licensing may be for you.

By empowering creators and developers to choose how their work is used, open licenses have helped create a vast store of free, publicly available knowledge, which anyone can contribute to and build off of, without fear of violating copyright or facing litigation. At the same time, artists, scientists and creators can more easily than ever share their work, and open licenses have enabled countless artists to reach audiences they might not have been able to otherwise. Projects like Wikipedia, Wiki-How and the Public Library of Science are made possible by the spirit of sharing and collaboration at the heart of the open licenses, and depend upon CC licenses to operate effectively.

THE BOTTOM LINE

For software there's GPL, LGPL, BSD, MIT, Apache and more; for everything else there's Creative Commons (CC).

GPL, LGPL, BSD, MIT, Apache and more: openly licensing software

Openly licensing your software enables you to grow users and encourage community involvement. Small teams can take advantage of the global open source community to fix bugs and build upon the shoulders of the programmers before them.

When it comes to open source software licensing, there is no shortage of licenses to choose from. Of the five most common open source licenses, GPL, LGPL, BSD, MIT and Apache, all five of the licenses allow commercial and derivative works, but each license differs in terms of things like attribution and source code distribution requirements. So you may want to make your choice based on those particular needs. It's also important to keep in mind that a huge part of open source software licensing is becoming part of a community. Each license tends to attract certain types of coders so you may want to spend some time exploring those communities and seeing where you feel most at home.

Now, there's not enough space in this book to cover everything about the open source software licenses, but you can find more information about Open Software Licenses on our website.[16]

One last thing: although CC is incredibly versatile and shares much of the same spirit as the open source software community, it should not be used for licensing software! CC licenses do not address the distribution of source code or patent rights, which are often important when using and integrating free software.

---

16 "Open Source Licensing Guide." New Media Rights, 12 Sept. 2008. Web. 23 Feb. 2016. <http://www. newmediarights.org/open_source/new_media_rights_open_source_licensing_guide>.

Creative Commons – open licensing for copyrighted content that isn't software.

So you'd like to use an open license for your work, now what? Most likely, you'll want to use one of the CC licenses (however, if you're looking to license software, you'll want to back track to our "GPL, LGPL, BSD, MIT, Apache and more: openly licensing software" section above). The CC license suite is essentially a set of flexible, pre-written, copyright licenses that provide a simple, standardized way to give the public permission to share and use a creative work, under certain conditions.

At first glance, deciphering what the various CC terms mean may seem intimidating, but in fact, it all comes down to the simple question of how you want your work to be used. Remember, offering your work under a CC license does not mean giving up your copyright. It means offering *some* of your rights to any member of the public, but only on certain conditions. Which conditions? Well, let's go through some questions you should ask yourself when choosing a CC license. This will help you pick the best license for your project.

One very important thing to keep in mind, however, is that CC licenses are non-revocable and non-exclusive. Non-exclusive means that the license is not restricted to one particular group or person. Non-revocable means that once you license a work under one kind of CC license, you can't take it back. You may choose to license the work under additional CC or custom licenses, but any time you've applied a CC license to a work, the work is permanently licensed under those terms. This is all to say it's very important to carefully consider how you want your work to be used when selecting your license.

Do you want to require people to give you credit for your work?

Every CC license requires something called "Attribution." This means that anyone using your CC licensed work is required to cite you as the original creator of the work. As a creator, you can choose to waive the attribution requirement, but by default the license itself tells the user to include the name of the original author, the title of the work, and a link to the legal code of the license. For some content creators, attribution may be all that they require. If, for example, you are an artist seeking to get your music out to the widest possible audience with the fewest limitations how it is reused, you would choose to license your work under a Creative Commons-Attribution (CC-BY) license. This is the most accommodating CC license in that it places the least number of restrictions possible on the person reusing your work. The CC-BY license allows the public to reuse and remix the work, even for commercial projects, and is not restricted in what license they choose for their derivative work.

Do you want to allow someone to reuse your work in a commercial project?

For some creators, the CC-BY license is a bit too generous and relinquishes too much control of the work. By choosing the Creative Commons-NonCommercial (CC-BY-NC) license, content creators permit remixing and reusing of the work, but forbid anyone from making commercial use of their work. Attribution is still required, and the public is permitted to remix, copy, distribute, display, and perform the work, but for noncommercial purposes only. This is an effective way for artists and creators (especially those who are new or emerging) to get their creative work to a larger audience, because the creative work can be redistributed non-commercially on noncommercial blogs, podcasts, social media websites, and elsewhere. Your photograph, song, story, or other creative work can gain the attention of the public, but it can't be used for an advertisement, sold by a record label, or turned into a television sitcom without your permission and compensation.

Do you want to allow someone to remix your work?

Derivative works are creative works that build upon previous works. Unless you indicate otherwise, CC licenses embrace the spirit of sharing at the heart of remix culture, and encourage the public to share and build upon your work. Artists and content creators can, by choosing a Creative Commons Attribution-NonDerivative (CC-BY-ND) license, forbid the modification of their work, while still allowing the public to share and reuse it. If you do not allow derivative works, then the only thing that can be distributed, copied, displayed, or performed is your exact original work. It's important to keep in mind that allowing derivative works does not necessarily mean anyone can profit off the work without your explicit permission. Even if you allow others to create a derivative work, they cannot exploit the song commercially if you have chosen to require uses to be "noncommercial," as discussed above.

Do you want to require that anyone using your work share his or her project similarly?

The final condition to consider is whether you would like to require that anyone using your work embrace the same spirit of sharing that you did by choosing a CC license. The "ShareAlike" requirement in a CC license requires that any use of your creative work carry the same exact licensing terms as you chose for your work. The "ShareAlike" requirement does, however, place some additional restrictions on the user of the content, because they have no choice in the licensing scheme for a work that incorporates your work. This term is intended to make sure derivative works created from your work are similarly open to share and build upon. Some creators will find this term restrictive. That said, if they want to use it under other terms, they could simply pay you for a license to use it.

Making your choice!

As you can see, although CC licenses can seem intimidating at first, in reality it all comes down to what license works best for you. Now that you've gone through those basic questions, it's time to mix and match to pick your license of choice! Hopefully the information above helped provide a clear answer as to what license to choose, but if not, CC has created a simple web app that can be used to help walk you through choosing a CC license.[17] Simply answer the questions by selecting the buttons that most accurately describe how you would like your work to be used, and the app does the rest, providing you with a proper license and HTML code that can be included wherever your content is published.

Best Practices for Reusing Creative Commons Content:

So, now you want to use someone else's openly licensed content. What's the best way to use their work appropriately? First and foremost, make sure that the way you are using the work complies with the terms of the license it is under! Be certain that if you are using work licensed under a CC-BY-NC or CC-BY-NC-SA license that your project is completely noncommercial. If there is a Sharealike requirement, know that you're going to have to license your derivative under the same license as the work you're using. If the work has a NoDerivative limitation, you ought to make sure that the work is being displayed completely, without any modifications.

The next thing to keep in mind is proper attribution. Always, always attribute the original author in the most reasonable way possible with the medium of your work. To properly attribute works that you reuse under a CC license, the general rule of thumb is to include in your attribution the acronym TASL, which stands for:

1. Title – What is the name of the material?

2. Author – Who owns the material?

---

17 "Choose a License." Creative Commons. Web. 23 Feb. 2016. <http://www.creativecommons.org/choose/>.

3. Source – Where can I find it?

4. License – What specific license is the work is under?

For example, Jerry may have licensed his photographs under a CC 4.0 Attribution - Noncommercial license. Proper attribution in that case would include the author's (Jerry's) name, a link or indication of where the original is located, and a note that the work is "used under Creative Commons Attribution-Non-Commercial 4.0 license." Since the release of Creative Commons 1.0, the attribution requirements have been modified slightly with each major release of the licenses suite. Version 4.0, the most recent release, has removed the explicit requirement to include the title of the work in your attribution, but if possible it is still considered best practice to do so. Whenever possible, include links to the license terms so others can easily access the information. More information on how to cite to specific mediums can be found on our website[18], but with the information in this chapter you should be ready to go out in the world and create and remix using open licenses.

---

18 Roane, Emory, and Teri Karobonik. "Best Practices for Creative Commons Attributions." New Media Rights, 12 Nov. 2015. Web. 23 Feb. 2016. <http://www.newmediarights.org/guide/how_to/creative_commons/best_practices_creative_commons_attributions>.

Chapter 10
I can Reuse Anything on the Internet, Right?
An introduction to Fair Use

By this point in the book you've probably figured out that copyright doesn't disappear on the internet and just because an image is on the internet doesn't mean it's free to use. That said there are ways to lawfully reuse copyrighted content without permission, primarily under a part of copyright law called fair use. In this chapter we'll explore: fair use, common fair use myths, fair use best practices, and the public domain.

Intro to Fair Use

THE BOTTOM LINE

Fair use, the free speech safety valve to copyright's monopoly, allows you to reuse others' copyrighted works without permission under certain circumstances based on a 4 factor balancing test. Although it's difficult to say with 100% certainty that something is fair use before a court decides the matter, having a good understanding of the fair use factors will help you make more informed decisions about reusing content.

What do *The Daily Show*, a Betamax VCR and your middle school book report all have in common? They are all examples of fair use. Fair use is a part of copyright law that allows you to reuse copyrighted works under certain circumstances without the permission of the copyright owner. This First Amendment safety valve to copyright law helps to ensure that speech and creativity isn't unduly suppressed while balancing the copyright owners' ability to profit from their work.

As you can imagine, an area of the law that is flexible enough to include *The Daily Show*, a Betamax VCR, and your middle school book report isn't cut and dry. Instead, fair use is a balancing test that requires balancing the following four factors:

5. Purpose and character of the use;

6. Nature of the original copyrighted work;

7. Amount and substance taken from the original work; and

8. Effect on the market value of the original.

It's important to learn about how each factor affects your fair use argument so you can reuse works safely. So without further ado let's jump right into the factors.

Factor One: Purpose and Character of the Use

This two-part factor tends to be the most important factor in deciding many fair use questions. The two key parts to be considered are:

1. Is the use commercial or noncommercial?

2. Is the use "transformative," that is, does it add new meaning or message to the original work?

In particular, the second part about whether the use is "transformative" is by far the most important piece of this factor, and can often make or break a fair use argument. We spend a good amount of time on transformation below.

Commercial/Non-commercial Use

In general, a non-commercial use is more likely to be fair use than a commercial one. Of course commercial uses fall on a wide spectrum, but in general if you're selling the work, or selling access to the work, it would be a commercial use. On the other end of the spectrum, if the use were truly a personal use without any economic benefit, it would be a non-commercial use. It's very important to remember that this is just one part of one factor in a much larger balancing test. Just because your use is non-commercial doesn't mean it is fair use, just as reusing a work commercially doesn't bar a finding of fair use.

Transformation

Although not defined within copyright law itself, transformation typically means to use or alter an original work such that it provides new meaning or message. The more you transform the original work to have a new voice, message, or meaning, the more likely it is to be transformative and the more likely it is to be fair use. Transformation might also involve physical alterations, but slight changes and edits by themselves are usually not transformative enough. So practically, what does transformation look like? Here are a few examples of transformative uses:

- **Buffy vs. Edward: Twilight Remixed by Jonathan McIntosh.**[19]

  This is a particularly great example of fair use because McIntosh takes a series of very small clips from the entire Buffy the Vampire Slayer TV series and mashes it together with tiny bits of the Twilight movie to create a new original story, changing the message of the original clips from stories about vampires to a cultural critique of gender roles in vampire pop culture.

- **Sorry for Partying T-Shirt by Sconnie Nation.**[20]

  In 2011, an apparel company reused a photo of Wisconsin mayor Paul Soglin to comment on his efforts to shut down Madison's annual "Mifflin Street Block Party," which the mayor himself had helped start while he was a student at the University of Wisconsin in 1969. The t-shirt (picture here[21]) is an excellent example of transformative use first, for taking the photo and heavily stylizing it in neon green in a way that the now conservative mayor would no doubt find unbefitting of a man of his stature. Second by adding the words "Sorry for partying," in a highly stylized party font, to comment on the mayor's change in opinion about the celebration.

- **"Pretty Woman" by 2 Live Crew.**

  The rap Group 2 Live Crew reused the guitar riff and some of the lyrics from Roy Orbison's "Oh Pretty Woman" to create a parody of the song. This particular parody is an excellent example of fair use not only because it, as the court put it, "juxtaposes the romantic musings of a man whose fantasy comes true, with degrading taunts, a bawdy demand

---

19 McIntosh, Jonathan. "Buffy vs Edward: Twilight Remixed -- [original Version]." YouTube. 19 June 2009. Web. 23 Feb. 2016. <https://youtu.be/RZwM3GvaTRM>.

20 Cullen, Sandy. "Judge Rules Soglin 'Sorry for Partying' Shirt Did Not Violate Copyright." Wisconsin State Journal, 16 Aug. 2013. Web. 23 Feb. 2016. <http://host.madison.com/wsj/news/local/crime_and_courts/judge-rules-soglin-sorry-for-partying-shirt-did-not-violate/article_87b1c317-a0ab-58d9-af52-aa360ea0f549.html>.

21 Ibid.

for sex and a sigh of relief for parental responsibility,"[22] but also because of the socio-economic and racial juxtaposition between the two songs.

Reusing something in a transformative way is critical to a finding of fair use! If your reuse isn't transformative it is highly unlikely that your use will be considered fair use unless all of the other factors are in your favor. We'll talk about fair use rules of thumb later on in the chapter, but for more examples of transformation you may want to check out our fair use resources page.[23]

Factor Two: The Nature of the Original Copyrighted Work

When it comes to the nature of the work we look at:

1. **Whether the work is factual or creative**

   Uses of works that are factual in nature are more likely to be fair use than uses of creative works because facts are not protected by copyright law.

2. **If the work is published or unpublished**

   Under this factor, reuse of unpublished works is less likely to be fair use because one of the rights granted to copyright owners is the decision if and when they would like to publish their work.

Factor Three: Amount and Substance Taken From the Original Work

This factor looks at how much of the original work you reused in your own work. You need to think about how much was used from both a quantitative and qualitative perspective. The three key questions are:

1. **How much of the original work did you reuse?**

   The more of a work that you reuse in your own work, the less likely it is to be fair use, so it's important to use only as much as you need to make your point. As we'll explain later, there is no magic number of seconds or percentage of a work that will always be fair use, so using just as much as you need to make your point is critical.

---

22 Campbell v. Acuff-Rose Music. 583. United States Supreme Court. 7 Mar. 1994.< https://www.law.cornell.edu/supct/html/92-1292.ZS.html>

23 "Fair Use Resources." New Media Rights, 23 July 2015. Web. 23 Feb. 2016. <http://www.newmediarights.org/fair_use_resources>.

2. How much did you take in relation to your work?

While it may be helpful that you only reused 30 seconds of footage, if your entire video consists only of those thirty seconds, it's much less likely to be fair use than a longer clip reused in a feature length documentary.

3. What did you take?

Not all parts of a work are necessarily equal when it comes to fair use. Using the "heart of the work" or the most critical part of the work is less likely to be fair use in most cases. So what parts of the work might be considered "the heart of the work"? Think of moments like the season finale of a reality TV show, the chorus of a song, or anything that might warrant a "spoiler alert."

Here's an example to tie these three questions together. Think about condensing a two-hour movie like *Castaway* into a five-minute clip: footage of Chuck crashing, finding and befriending Wilson, building the raft, going out to sea, losing Wilson, then being saved. The clip is a shallow imitation of the movie, but it is substantial and the core plot has survived. Despite its brevity, this use would not likely be fair use because it takes the "heart of the work" and reuses it without any additional commentary.

Parody

If you're reusing part of a work as a parody, you actually have significantly more leeway in using not only more of the work but the heart of the work as well. This is because for a parody to work your audience needs to know what you're making fun of or the entire thing falls apart. But before you take parody into account as part of your analysis, it's very important to know what a parody actually is. A parody is when you use a copyrighted work to make fun of the copyrighted work itself. For example, Weird Al's "Smell's Like Nirvana"[24] uses Nirvana's "Smells Like Teen Spirit"[25] to make fun of the song itself, particularly how incoherent the original Nirvana song was. This makes it a great example of a parody. This is very different from satire, which uses a copyrighted work to make fun of something unrelated to that copyrighted work. For example, Weird Al's "Word Crimes,"[26] which uses the

---

24 "Smells Like Nirvana" Perf. "Weird Al" Yankovic. YouTube. 2 Oct. 2009. Web. 23 Feb. 2016. <https://youtu.be/FklUAoZ6KxY>.

25 Smells Like Teen Spirit. Perf. Nirvana. YouTube. 16 June 2009. Web. 23 Feb. 2016. <https://youtu.be/hTWKbfoikeg>.

26 Word Crimes. Perf. "Weird Al" Yankovic. YouTube. 15 July 2015. Web. 23 Feb. 2016. <https://youtu.be/8Gv0H-vPoDc>.

song "Blurred Lines"[27] to make fun of the atrociously bad grammar found online, is a great example of satire because it is not directly making fun of "Blurred Lines" itself. Satire is not given the same type of leeway and in fact reusing something as part of a satire can be much trickier under fair use. If you're reusing a work as part of a satire you'll need to reuse much less of the work or get permission to reuse the work.

Factor Four: The Effect On the Market Value of the Original

This factor focuses on how your new use affects the value of the original work, and the potential (or actual) market for the original work. The more your work serves as a substitute for the original, the less likely it qualifies as fair use. The more adverse the effect on the market for the original (including the market for "derivative" works, adaptations of the original), the less likely your use qualifies as fair use.

While a particular use of another's content may arguably be fair use, it is impossible to guarantee that a court would come out the same way because reasonable minds may differ on how the factors should be balanced. If you'd like to walk through the fair use factors in a more interactive way, check out our fair use app.[28]

Fair Use Myths

There are a lot of myths about fair use out there. In this section we'll try to debunk the top nine myths about fair use.

4.   **Myth: Any journalistic, educational, research use or use for commentary is automatically fair use.**

    Truth: No category of work is ever categorically fair use. Although many point to the list in the preamble of 17 USC 107 of different types of uses including "criticism, comment, news reporting, teaching (including multiple copies for classroom use), scholarship, or research," this entire list is just a list of the categories of uses where fair use has a tendency to show up. That's it. It's just a flag to indicate the potential existence of fair use in certain cases; much like a road sign warning of falling rocks indicates that rocks may fall on the road, it doesn't necessarily mean there will always be rocks on the road ahead.

---

27   Blurred Lines. Perf. Robin Thicke Featuring T.I. and Pharrell. YouTube. 20 Mar. 2013. Web. 23 Feb. 2016. <https://youtu.be/yyDUC1LUXSU>.

28   "The Fair Use App." New Media Rights, 15 July 2015. Web. 23 Feb. 2016. <http://newmediarights.org/fairuse/>.

5. **Myth: Any use of a copyrighted work for non-commercial use is ok.**

   Truth: While a non-commercial use is more likely to be fair use, it isn't a guarantee that it will be. Commercial vs. non-commercial use is only a small part of the analysis.

6. **Myth: If a work hasn't been published yet it can't be protected.**

   Truth: As we explain above, unpublished works are actually more protected by copyright law and less likely to be fair use because only the copyright owner has the right to decide when and even if a work is published.

7. **Myth: If I only use ¼, 20% or 20 seconds of the work or less it will automatically be fair use!**

   Truth: There is no set amount that will always be fair use; fair use is fundamentally a balancing test, which isn't consistent with bright line rules like these.

8. **Myth: I gave attribution therefore my use is fair use.**

   Truth: Attribution, while helpful and polite, is not a part of the fair use factors or legal analysis in any way.

9. **Myth: I put the fair use statute 17 U.S.C. §107 on my work, therefore its fair use.**

   Truth: Your ability to copy and paste statutory language is not a part of the fair analysis and will likely have no legal effect whatsoever.

10. **Myth: Getting to reuse this work is morally fair and that's enough.**

    Truth: Fair use is a bit of a misnomer in this regard. It really doesn't have anything to do with what is fair, moral or necessarily right. Instead, it really comes back to the fair use factors.

11. **Myth: Fair use is only a tool for dirty pirates; real business people don't use fair use.**

    Truth: Fair use is a critical tool for everyone, including many legitimate businesses and commercial entities like The Daily Show. Even the Motion Picture Association of America has supported fair use repeatedly, although their view of fair use is rather narrow.[29] Fair use remains a critical safety valve that allows speech to flourish, especially among legitimate business.

12. **Myth: Fair use is so unpredictable, so it doesn't exist in practice.**

Truth: There's a reason that the stereotypical lawyer answer is "it depends." At the very core of our legal system is a series of laws that are applied based on a series of facts. So while many answers are possible, it is possible to prepare the best fair use argument possible and proceed based on that argument, much like you would in any other area of law.

Fair Use Rules of Thumb

So we've talked about the fair use factors and some fair use myths. Although there are no black and white rules when it comes to fair use, in this section we'll lay out some fair use rules of thumb to help you apply the fair use factors effectively.

- **Use just as much as you need to make your point**

  Think back to middle school for a moment, back to when you first learned to quote a source in an essay. Your teacher probably told you that you should only quote as much as you need to make your point both to craft a better argument, but also not to overly inflate your paper with stuff that only padded your page count. When you're reusing something in fair use you'll want to draw upon that same skill set and reuse only the material that helps you make your point.

- **Provide credit where credit is due**

  Although providing attribution has no legal effect, it can have a very big practical one. Many copyright owners are most upset, not that their work was reused in fair use, but that it was reused without giving them credit. Keep in mind that even when you're in the right about fair use, a copyright owner may still make a big stink about the fact that they weren't given credit, and providing this credit can be a good way of staving off an argument that doesn't need to happen.

---

29 Sheffner, Ben. "MPAA and Fair Use: A Quick History." Policy Focus An in Depth Look at Policies and Positions. MPAA, 22 Oct. 2013. Web. 23 Feb. 2016. <http://www.mpaa.org/mpaa-and-fair-use-a-quick-history/>.

- **Use a wide variety of sources**

  The logic on this one is pretty simple. The more sources you draw from, the less likely it is you'll draw too much from any one source, making your uses more likely to be fair use.

- **Don't rely on fair use for filler**

  Whether you're a filmmaker looking for b-roll or a blogger looking for a stock photo, using a piece of copyrighted content for its aesthetic effect is unlikely to be fair use.

Be especially wary when reusing music. For a variety of reasons, the law surrounding fair use and music has developed on a bit of an alternate track from the rest of fair use law. Meaning that unless you're specifically discussing a song or parodying a song, it is very unlikely to be fair use. However, there <u>are a number of sources</u> that have top notch openly licensed or royalty free music that you can use at low to no cost.[30]

Again, while these rules of thumb are not bright line rules, they can help you make smarter decisions about fair use.

Public Domain

Although sometimes confused with fair use, the public domain consists of works that are no longer protected by copyright and does not concern itself with the reuse of copyrighted works. In this part of the chapter we'll try to debunk some of the top myths about the public domain, to help you learn more about reusing works in the public domain.

- **Myth: If I found it on the internet/Twitter, Facebook it's in the public domain.**

  Truth: copyright law doesn't end on the internet.
  Posting something online, even on social media, doesn't push something into the public domain.

- **Myth: If it was created before 1923 it's always in the public domain.**

  Truth: Not necessarily. Although many works published before 1923 are in the public domain, there are a handful of holdouts.

30 "How to Find Free Music, Images, and Video You Can Use or Remix in Your Own Creative Works." New Media Rights, 18 Feb. 2009. Web. 23 Feb. 2016. <http://www.newmediarights.org/guide/how_to/social_media/social_video/find_free_music_images_video_use_remix_creative_works>.

Most notably because sound recordings were not protected by federal law until the 1976 Copyright Act, no sound recordings will enter the public domain until February 15th 2067 (unless the state it was recorded in places it in the public domain). For help figuring out if something is in the public domain, we recommend checking out this awesome chart from Cornell here.[31]

- **Myth: It doesn't have a copyright symbol on it; I can use it because it's in the public domain.**
  Truth: Although putting a copyright notice on a work used to be required, this requirement was phased out by March 1st 1989. A copyright notice is not required for a work to be protected by copyright. Although not a requirement, for online creators it can still be helpful to put the copyright symbol near your work to avoid confusion, particularly given how prevalent this myth is.

- **Myth: It was never registered; it's in the public domain.**
  Truth: Although registering your copyright with the US Copyright Office used to be required, this requirement was phased out by March 1st 1989. Although registration can be helpful, it is not required for a work to be protected by copyright.

- **The author is dead or it's really old, so it must be public domain.**
  Truth: Copyright protection lasts for the author's lifetime plus 70 years, or for works produced by companies the shorter of 95 years from publication or 120 years from creation. Therefore just because an author is dead or a work is very old doesn't mean a work is in the public domain.

- **If it's out of print it's public domain.**
  Truth: Because copyright protection lasts so long, there are many works that are out of print but have not passed into the public domain. For this reason, it's actually easier to find a book for sale from the 1880's than the 1980's because sorting out who owns the rights to a particular book can be especially tricky.[32]

---

31 "Copyright Term and the Public Domain in the United States." Cornell Copyright Information Center. Web. 23 Feb. 2016. <http://copyright.cornell.edu/resources/publicdomain.cfm>.
32 Heald, Paul J. "How Copyright Makes Books and Music Disappear (and How Secondary Liability Rules Help Resurrect Old Songs)." SSRN Electronic Journal SSRN Journal. Web. 23 Feb. 2016. <http://papers.ssrn.com/sol3/papers.cfm?abstract_id=2290181>.

- **If it was created by the government, it's in the public domain.**
  Truth: If a work was created by an employee of the federal government as part of their duties, then that work is in the public domain. However, state and local governments are free to make their own rules about which of their works are subject to copyright protection.
  Also, remember that even if an individual is a current federal, state, or local government official, if a work is created as part of their separate efforts or as a candidate for political office, then it is protected by copyright and is not a government work. So in that case you'll need to rely on fair use or a license to reuse the work.

- **I can't put my work in the public domain.**
  Truth: Although there is no formal legal tool to do so, using the Creative Commons public domain designation, CC0, is as close as you can get to legally placing your work in the public domain. You can learn more about that option here![33]

In this chapter, we've provided a brief overview of fair use. But fair use can be a tricky area even for experienced creators. We always recommend that if you have questions about fair use you should ask an experienced copyright attorney for help.

---

33 "About CC0 — "No Rights Reserved"." Creative Commons. Web. 23 Feb. 2016. <http://creativecommons. org/about/cc0>.

Chapter 11
Is it Really an Endorsement if I'm not a Celebrity? What you Need to Know About Disclaimers.

Free stuff is awesome. Whether it's free massages at an event or a company giving you free items to blog about, we all love free stuff. But when you write or make videos about the free stuff you get, there could be consequences if you don't take the proper precautions. In this chapter we'll break down how to avoid false advertising claims by using disclaimers and some of the unique things you need to know about using disclaimers online.

Why would you need a disclaimer in the first place?

In 1980, the Federal Trade Commission (FTC) created a series of guidelines to protect consumers from faulty and misleading advertisements. Advertisements can affect the way consumers choose to buy certain products and services. Without regulation, consumers could purchase products and services that do not work as expected. With the development of technology this century, the FTC now applies these guidelines to podcasts, vlogs, blogs, social media and other online media because they often contain advertisements. If a user relies on information in a podcast or blog as your opinion and not a paid advertisement you could face an enforcement action from the FTC. Therefore, having a disclaimer helps your users interpret when your work is and is not an advertisement.

Ok, but when do I need to use disclaimers?

THE BOTTOM LINE

If you're getting something for free in a way that could sway the way you talk about a product or service; you should have a clear and conspicuous disclosure.

You don't always need to have disclaimer when you mention a product or service on your blog. If you purchased a product or service on your own, got a discount that was available to everyone or received a giveaway item that was publicly available, then you don't need to include a disclaimer. Why? Because even if you got a great deal, it doesn't affect the weight your readers may give to your recommendation.

On the other hand, when you are advocating for a certain product or service because you received compensation for that opinion or are getting some benefit not available to the public, you will need a disclaimer. Keep in mind that the FTC thinks about compensation very broadly even if the item you receive isn't a big ticket item (such as a BOGO coupon or even a tiny packet of moisturizer) or it's an experience (the chance to appear in a commercial, get invited to exclusive parties, getting a one month free lease on a car), you still need to disclose it because getting it for free could affect your opinion of the product or service. Here are a few more specific examples of situations you may need to use a disclaimer:

- Mandy receives a free makeup set from a popular makeup brand as part of their "ambassador program" so she can vlog about it. Mandy needs to include a disclaimer in her video that she was given the makeup by the makeup brand.

- Bob is a blogger. A local technology company paid him $300 to blog about their new delivery drone. Bob must include a disclaimer in his blog that he was paid to write the article.

- Chris has a travel podcast. On his most recent stay at a hotel, the manager comped his entire stay and said, "Anything for you Chris! We love your podcast and we hope you'll consider showing us some love in your next episode." Even though Chris was prepared to pay for his stay, the gift of a free room could alter his opinion of the hotel and he must include a specific disclosure in his next podcast if he talks about the hotel.

- Marsha, a videogame blogger, gets invited to try out a new videogame at EA's offices. EA loans her a copy of the game for two weeks so she can review it. Regardless of the content of Marsha's review, because she received the game for free she will need to include a disclosure in her blog post.

- Clark attends a star-studded awards show and receives one of their famous swag bags filled with certificates for tropical vacations, pricey tech goodies, and gift cards for insanely expensive restaurants. Clark, a non-celebrity blogger who was a +1 to his industry friend, may need to disclose in his review of his tropical vacation that he got it for free in a swag bag because of the exclusive and over-the-top nature of this particular swag bag.

And here are a few examples where you would not need a disclaimer:

- Sandy mentions several products on her blog that she bought on sale with a coupon she found online during a recent shopping trip. Even if Sandy got a killer deal, because these deals were available to the general public, no disclaimer is required.

- Bob talks about the delicious free-sample lunch he had at Costco. Since the free samples were available for all customers, no disclosure is required.

- Chris goes to a conference and, like all other attendees, gets a swag bag at check-in filled with snacks, stickers and a pack of branded playing cards. Because this bag was available to all attendees Chris doesn't need to include a disclosure if he reviews something that was in the bag.

Ok, I need a disclaimer. What should my disclaimer look like?

Time for your least favorite lawyer answer: it depends. It depends on what you need to disclose and what platform you are using. The general rule is that disclosures must be "clear and conspicuous," but before we get into some specific examples of what that might look like, here are some general principals to help you make clear and conspicuous disclosures:

13. **Your disclosure shouldn't be in legalese.**

    When it comes to effective advertising disclosures, plain, simple, easy to understand language is best. When it comes to social media, even using the #Ad may be sufficient to indicate that something is an advertisement; particularly on platforms where you have a limited character count.

14. **Your disclosure should be complete.**

    It may not be enough to say that you got something for free, particularly if you were given additional compensation on top of the free item to ensure your positive review. Be sure to disclose anything that could bias your review of a product.

15. **The disclosure must be near the relevant content.**

Having one disclosure at the top of your web page or a link to a disclosure isn't enough. It needs to be conspicuous to the average viewer of your content. That means it needs to be near the content.

16. **The disclosure should be easy to read and stand out from the background.**

Your disclosure is not the time to bust out size nine, light yellow, Wingding font.

17. **If you have a written ad on a video, it must be on the screen long enough for a viewer to notice it, read it and understand it.**

18. **Audio disclosure should be spoken at a normal pace, so that your listener can understand it.**

19. **Even if you use a disclaimer you must tell the truth!**

Remember a disclaimer isn't a get-out-of-false-advertising-claims-free card. Even if you make a disclaimer, your review should be as truthful as possible. This doesn't mean your negative reviews need to be mean, stream of conscious rants. But it does mean you should shy away from making untrue statements, like saying a product worked great when it didn't even turn on.

Example Disclaimers

- Referring back to the YouTube example from above, if a beauty company did pay you or gave you the product for free in exchange for the YouTube review, then this should be disclosed. You could include this specific disclaimer orally or in writing at the beginning of the clip with words like "[insert beauty company name] gave me this [insert hair care product] for free so that I could demonstrate its quality to my users."

- Back to Bob the blogger. A local technology company paid him $300 to blog about their new delivery drone. Bob must include a disclaimer in his blog that he was paid to write the article. Bob may want to include as his first sentence or as a subheading to the article something like "sponsored post" above his blog, or should start his blog with a sentence like "I received payment from [insert company name]. to write this blog"

- Anne is a part of a lifestyle brands blogger network. After trying out the yoga mat she was given through the network, she wants to tweet about it. She might try tweeting "Loving my new yoga mat from Yoga Stars! Didn't slip once in my hot yoga class #Ad"

Samantha has a Twitch live stream channel. A videogame company gave her an advance copy of their new game to live stream and a t-shirt to wear during the stream. While playing, Samantha should periodically make oral disclosures that she received the game and the T-shirt for free from the videogame company.

Other times when you might need a disclaimer.

Disclaimers aren't necessarily all about free stuff. There are a few other types of situations where you may need subject-specific disclaimers.

- Selling medicine, health, beauty or fitness products or services.

- Political advertising.

- Selling physical products. Certain types of physical products like jewelry may have their own disclosure requirements. In addition, if you'd like to advertise your product as made in the USA, there are specific guidelines you must follow.

- Professional advertising. Depending on your profession, like lawyers or CPAs, you may have certain disclaimers you must use for your online advertising and content.

Since most of these types of disclaimers involve specific areas of law, you should to talk to a lawyer about writing a disclaimer narrowly tailored to your needs.

While disclaimers can be a confusing area, hopefully this chapter helped give you a nice grounding in the basics of disclaimers. Now go forth and get your swag on!

Chapter 12
Why you Should Care About Being Accurate and Truthful

Some of the best independent journalism projects, bloggers, filmmakers, early stage nonprofits, and artists create work that shines a light onto the practices of the most powerful individuals, businesses and governments in our world. But shining this light requires being accurate with the information that is published online. This is true even if you're just using social media or writing online. In this chapter we'll explore the legal concept of defamation and provide you with helpful ways to avoid it in your work and social media.

Defamation & False Light

THE BOTTOM LINE

Defamation protects people from the harm that can come from other people lying about them verbally or in text. A statement is defamatory when it is a false statement of fact. So remember, no matter how much you believe it to be true, calling someone a "pretentious grumpy pants" is an opinion, not defamation.

To begin, let's look at the point where statements normally protected under free speech cross into defamation land. Generally speaking, defamation occurs when:

- Someone makes a false statement that is harmful to another's reputation;

- The statement appears to convey a fact, not just an opinion;

- It is published or communicated to a third person (online posting counts)

- The person making the statement is at fault because they or someone under their control, like an employee, made the statement

- The subject of the statement is harmed as a result.

If the statement is a public figure the person making the statement knows the statement is false but makes it any way. Consider the following example: John, suspicious of his co-worker, Jane, but knowing he has no evidence of any wrongdoing, goes on Twitter and tweets, "Jane Doe has embezzled thousands of dollars of company funds." Several people read the statement, including Jane's boss, who soon after decides to let Jane go. Now jobless, Jane spends months frantically trying to repair her reputation and find new work. Suppose that John was mistaken, and Jane had never actually embezzled money.

Jane would have a strong claim for defamation against John because: (1) John made a false statement about Jane that hurt her reputation because she did not actually embezzle money, and the statement affected her boss' opinion of her; (2) the statement appeared to convey a fact because there was no indication that John was voicing his opinion about Jane's actions, or that he was joking; (3) the statement was published to a third party because it was posted online where several people read it, including Jane's boss; (4) John was at fault because he used incorrect information knowing that it had no factual basis whatsoever; (5) Jane was harmed financially because she lost an important source of income, and possibly emotionally from any mental anguish caused by John's false statement.

In contrast, imagine John tweeted the following, "Jane Doe is a pretentious grumpy pants." Although this statement may be hurtful to Jane, calling someone a "pretentious grumpy pants" is a matter of opinion and not an objectively provable fact; thus this tweet would not be defamatory.

Defamation vs. libel vs. slander

Defamation, libel, and slander all get bandied about and many people don't know that each of these terms means something different. Below we'll break the differences down for you.

Defamation: A false statement of fact made about another person in a public setting that causes harm.

Libel: Written or published defamation.

Slander: Oral defamation.

Implying false things

It's important to keep in mind that just because you don't make a factual statement, doesn't mean you don't have to worry about being accurate. Some states have "false light" laws, which prohibit the publication of something that places someone in a false light that would be highly offensive to a reasonable person. Unlike defamation, false light it doesn't need to involve a factual statement. Consider the following example: John is an investigative journalist writing a blog about shoplifting. John needs an image to use with his blog. John decides to use his photo of two older women in a mall and places it under the headline "Shoplifting into retirement: how stagnant social security is turning seniors into shoplifters." Madge and Barbara, the women in the photo, may have a pretty good claim for false light because by placing their photo next to that particular headline he implied that they were shoplifters and placed them in a false light.

Best practices for being accurate and truthful online and in your work.

As we all become content producers whether on social media, blogs or even films, the risk of making a defamatory statement continues to grow. There are many examples of lawsuits brought over short social media posts. Below, we provide some helpful tips for keeping you out of trouble when producing content. While some of the suggestions might seem basic, they can go a long way towards avoiding unwanted legal trouble.

1. **Think carefully about what you're writing or saying.**

   Before you post, tweet, or publish, take a second to read it over. Then, consider how it might affect someone's reputation. It might be useful to ask yourself, "How would a reasonable person interpret this?" If the message clearly targets the reputation of a particular person or group, it might be wise to revise it. Particularly if you know what you're saying isn't true.

2. **Be specific.**

   It is important to avoid ambiguity where possible. The last thing you want is for an angry reader to accuse you of saying something that you never intended in the first place. For example, suppose you post the following statement: "The Big Bacon Burger at Bob's Tavern = emergency room. It's baaaadd!!" While it may seem innocuous, several meanings can be implied here. The statement could be a hyperbole, meant to emphasize just how filling and delicious the Big Bacon Burger is, but it could also mean that the "Big Bacon Burger" *literally* causes food poisoning and will result in a trip to the hospital. Interpreted this way, the post may be considered defamatory. Make every character count in order to avoid ambiguity.

3. **Don't post anything when you're angry or emotional.**

Many of us say and do things we don't mean, especially in the heat of the moment. If you're feeling fired up, wait until you've cooled off and are thinking clearly before posting. A few extra minutes could go a long way towards preventing backlash from disgruntled readers, and avoiding time-consuming lawsuits.

4. **If it looks like a fact... make sure it's actually true.**

At the heart of every strong defamation claim is a factual statement that turns out to be false. With that in mind, it's not enough to *believe* what you're saying is true, the information should also come from a reliable source. For example, if you suspected that an online author used copyrighted content without permission in his latest article, you wouldn't want to create a YouTube video about how he "infringed his material" unless you had the facts to back it up. To help back your point up, you might also consider citing to source material if it's available.

5. **Make it clear when a statement is opinion or joke rather than fact.**

In order to avoid having your opinion mistaken for fact, try prefacing statements with language that clearly tells the reader that your message is opinion-based. For instance, instead of calling the leader of a Wall Street investment corporation a "corrupt businessman" or a "thief," begin the sentence with "I think," or "it seems." Ideally, you should still specify which true facts provide the basis for your opinion, i.e., "I think that he's a thief because he has made billions of dollars from the retirement funds of the public employees he claims to protect."

If you post material that makes a joke about a person or business, consider whether the average reader would be able to tell you are joking; if they could mistake your joke for fact, it's probably better not to post it. Also, keep in mind that on social media in particular folks are likely to read your post quickly, so a joke that would otherwise be okay could still be problematic if a quick skim wouldn't reveal it to be a joke.

6. **Avoid making criminal allegations or associating people with terrorist or hate groups.**

   If you accuse someone of a crime or associate them with an undesirable group such as a terrorist or hate group, you need to have strong evidence that they committed that crime or are associated with that group. It tends to be safer to talk about their conduct, rather than to label it. For instance, instead of saying "Bob Smith committed fraud," highlight the facts that you know for sure, i.e., "Bob Smith was misleading when he assured customers they would get their money back." Similarly, identifying a police officer as a "Neo-Nazi," or "white nationalist" should be based on specific evidence to support such claims. Otherwise, simply explain the facts as accurately as you know them, for instance, if it was the case that the officer "brutally injured an African American during a recent arrest."

7. **Be cautious when writing about private citizens.**

   Generally, the law is less forgiving when you write about private citizens than it is for public figures. Even if you were just careless or negligent in making a defamatory post about a private citizen and didn't realize the statement was false, you could be liable. For statements you make about public figures, the law provides a bit more protection. Typically you're only responsible for *knowingly* making a false statement, or *recklessly disregarding* the truth of the statement (*i.e. the facts were available but you actively avoided looking at them before posting*).

8. **Be careful when using hashtags!**

   It's possible that adding a hashtag to a tweet or other social media post could alter the context of the original message enough to make it defamatory. For example, if you tweeted out "Actor 'Mike Jones' was arrested on Tuesday for domestic violence," the statement would be perfectly acceptable so long as the arrest actually took place. However, if you added the hashtag "#rapist," the statement could now be considered false and possibly defamatory. Using something like hashtag "#Speakup," could help call attention to the issue while minimizing liability on your end. Also it's a very good idea to search a hashtag before adding it to the end of your post, just in case that hashtag has taken on a new and offensive meaning.

9. **Avoid modifying photos & videos in order to portray a person or business in a negative light.**

It's common to come across viral photos and videos that have been modified in order to make someone look bad. While some of these are funny and harmless, the same can't be said for others. Generally speaking, the less obvious and absurd the changes are, the more likely they will be considered defamatory. For example, suppose you want to create an internet meme by modifying an image of a popular athlete. If you altered the image to depict the athlete wearing a diaper and holding a rattle, it may be acceptable as a parody. In contrast, consider an image that depicts a popular athlete holding hands with his wife. If the image were distorted to make it appear that he was beating his wife, it could now be considered defamatory. If you're looking to expose a person for unlawful or immoral activity, stick to original images and unaltered footage.

10. **Chose appropriate thumbnails for your online videos.**

Thumbnail photos can be helpful in piquing a viewer's interest in a video that you have created. Because they are the first images people see before clicking "play," thumbnail photos should not only be relevant to video content, but should also reflect their messages. For example, a photo of a celebrity who has admittedly undergone numerous plastic surgeries may be an appropriate thumbnail for a video that sheds light on cosmetic surgery addiction, whereas a photo of a random man in a park would not be an appropriate thumbnail for a video about child abduction because it could show him in a false light by implying he is a kidnapper or worse.

11. **Be very careful when using stock photos.**

Stock photos typically come in two versions: those with model releases and those without. Using a photo of a human with a model release will typically protect you from false light or defamation claims because most model releases have models waive the right to bring those types of claims. If you use a stock photo without a model release the model still could bring a false light claim if your use of the photo puts them in a false light. For example let's say you use a stock photo of a man in a suit walking down the steps of a bank next to the headline "D.C. Banker Accused of Insider Trading." The model in the stock photo did not sign a model release. The man in the photo may have a pretty good claim for false light because by putting his photo under a headline about insider trading, the article seems to be implying that he was the banker accused of insider trading.

While it might seem like a lot of information to remember at first, the main idea is rather simple: it's best to take a careful and measured approach when expressing your thoughts and opinions online. Understanding the types of content that could be problematic can go a long way towards avoiding unwanted legal trouble.

Chapter 13
Privacy Law Still Exists: Avoiding Violating People's Privacy With What you Post Online

The internet is awesome! It lets you stay connected and allows you to share all of your creative projects with the click of a button. While posting online can be a great way to expose the world to your work, it's important to avoid over-exposing your clients, people whom you may have captured on film, and other folks because doing so could violate their privacy rights. In this chapter we'll discuss some common situations where privacy law can come into play and provide practical steps you can take to protect others privacy rights when you're creating. What we won't do in this chapter is discuss privacy policies and how to notify your users properly. For information on that you'll want to head back to Chapter 7.

What if I Want to Record Someone?

Whether you're a documentary filmmaker or a small guerilla marketing firm, odds are at some point you'll want to record, photograph or film someone else, which you may or may not need permission to do. Determining whether or not you can record someone depends a lot on the circumstances of the recording. Let's take a look at some typical scenarios where you may want to record someone and what steps you'll need to take to protect yourself.

Crowds

Let's say you are making a documentary and filming a large crowd of people at a public event. If a person briefly appears in the background or their back is turned away from the camera, you generally don't need consent to film them. However, if a person is clearly shown in the film, it is always a good idea to get a written release signed by them to protect against any invasion of privacy claims.

But what happens when getting a release isn't a workable solution? For example, what if you're filming a non-profit's annual fundraising event for an online ad campaign and they won't let you get written releases at the door? You might try putting up a public filming notice sign and film the sign to make a record of where it was posted. The sign will put the crowd on notice that they are being filmed and by being at the event, they are consenting to being filmed. Another great tip is to make a public announcement at the event notifying the audience that filming is taking place.

Interviewing someone

Suppose you want to interview someone for your documentary.
You will definitely want to get a written and signed interview release from the person you are interviewing. These are very useful because you can tailor the releases to fit your needs. You should always consult an attorney to make sure your written release has everything that you need in it because there are a lot of bad releases floating around the internet and using a release that isn't tailored to your needs can create huge problems for you later down the line.

In addition to getting a written release, it is also a good idea to get a verbal recording of that release. Before the interview even starts, state the purpose of the interview on camera and then explain the release to the person being interviewed, being careful not to contradict anything in the written release. Once you have explained the release, which might take a little bit of extra time, get their verbal agreement. This extra step will ensure that the person being interviewed was completely in the loop and knew what they were agreeing to in case things don't go as planned down the road.

What if I Want to Secretly Record Someone Speaking?

It is illegal for you to secretly record confidential conversations without the consent of parties to those conversations. How much consent do you need? Unfortunately this is another one of those questions where our answer is, it depends. In California, "two-party" consent is required, meaning that you would need to get consent from all parties you are recording. However, some states only require "one-party" consent. This means that you can record so long as you are a party to the conversation. Before you decide to record someone secretly, you should consult with an attorney in your state to find out if you are in a single-party or two-party consent state.

What happens if you don't get consent? In most states, secretly filming someone without their consent could carry heavy fines and even criminal damages, so it's absolutely critical to make sure you have gotten the proper consent!

Are there any additional legal risks associated with privacy that I should know about?

Whenever you use another person in your project and you share it with others, you run the risk of invading their privacy. Let's take a look at a couple of other situations where, if you aren't careful, you might invade someone else's privacy.

Shhhh! It's a Secret!

Let's be honest! Everyone loves getting to know a juicy secret! They are fun and exciting, until they are told to someone you don't want knowing. You cannot share your recording with others, especially online, if the recording contains private or secret facts about another person and sharing would be highly offensive to a reasonable person. There is an exception that if the publication is of genuine public concern and has some social value, then it can be shared. In other words, posting an audio recording of your former friend's run-in with the IRS in retaliation of a failed friendship is not of genuine public concern. However, writing a news article based on a secretly recorded company earnings call (from a single-party consent state) where the CEO makes a series of offensive remarks about the poor would be of public concern and will not lead to liability.

Get off my lawn, you crazy kids!

Sometimes to get the story, you may need to do a bit of digging. But if you're digging into other people's private property without their permission, it could lead to a whole host of liability from trespassing to privacy crimes to even potentially violating the Computer Fraud and Abuse Act. Although some of these laws have "public interest" exceptions, if you're planning a project that is based on exploring the private physical and digital lives of individuals, you'll want to contact an attorney to make sure you're staying on the right side of the law.

Meme worthy privacy invasions!

Everyone loves a good meme, but can a meme invade someone's privacy? If your meme places someone in a false light by maliciously implicating they're something they're not, you could run into trouble. For example, let's say you took a photo of a work colleague standing alone near the playground at a company picnic and used it to create a meme implying that he was a pedophile. By falsely implicating that your co-worker is a pedophile you could be placing him in a false light. For best practices to avoid false light claims flip back to Chapter 12.

Step 1 Endorsement, Step 2… Step 3 Profit, Step 4 Lawsuit?!?!?

Using endorsements can be a great way to sell a product, whether your endorsement comes from a celebrity or the average Joe. But you need to make sure you have permission from the individual who is endorsing your project, or risk violating their right of publicity. Let's suppose you use a picture of Jillian Michaels, the celebrity personal trainer for *The Biggest Loser*, in your commercial to advertise your new super healthy shakes and state, "Jillian never leaves home without one!" This could land you into trouble if you don't have permission to use her image and it could get you into even more trouble if the statement you make isn't true. You could also violate someone's right of publicity by putting their image on a product. For example, selling a T-shirt with a celebrity's face emblazoned on it could violate their right of publicity. That said, there are some First Amendment exceptions to the right of publicity. So if your primary goal is to report news involving an individual, create a parody product, or film a documentary about a matter of public concern, you may not need permission.

Also, keep in mind that in many states, this right of publicity extends past the death of an individual, so in many cases using dead people to sell your products or selling products with picture of dead people on them is not a viable right of publicity loophole. If you would like to use the likeness of someone who's passed away, you should look to his or her heirs for permission. You may also want to check in with a lawyer since the right of publicity after death varies greatly from state to state.

We hope this chapter has provided you with some guidance as to the appropriate ways you can use someone else's image or information online. When in doubt, it is always a good idea to check with a local attorney to make sure you're on the right side of privacy law.

Chapter 14
How to Watch Your Back While You're Making the Deal

THE BOTTOM LINE

You have a lot of options for distributing your work, whether it's a video series, film, song, book or video game. Pre-internet, you typically handed over most or all of your rights to a distributor, but it's becoming far more common to split up the rights or even self-distribute. While it's nice to have more choices, it means creators and entrepreneurs have to be savvy dealmakers. When an opportunity comes your way, take a deep breath and read the fine print before you break out the champagne.

Making a deal for all the rights to your creative work

This is the most traditional way for creators to share their work with the world. Back in the days when there were a more limited number of distribution channels through radio, television, book publishers, and movie theatres, you basically had to rely on another company to get your work in front of the public. If you were an established creator with a good reputation, you might have been able to command a good price for your work. New creators just starting out sometimes gave away all the rights to their work in return for very little.

If you get an offer for an assignment or exclusive license of your creative work for long periods of time ("perpetually"), it's ok to be excited, but also be wary. What do you get in return? Getting your film picked up by a major distributor, or your song picked up by a big record company could mean a lot of exposure and/or money, but neither is guaranteed. Once you do a long term deal for most or all of the rights to your work, money and exposure are largely out of your hands.

Do the math, and figure out if the amount you're being paid is worth giving all the rights to the other party. Even if the money is sufficient, does the other party have any requirements to actually try to get your work in front of audiences? If the idea is to use the success of this work to fund your next project, then the other party should be making real promises about what they are going to do to make sure audiences can access your work.

Splitting up the rights

Instead of giving the rights to your work to one distributor, why not split those rights up? Each creative project is different, so the audience and methods of distribution for each project could vary as well. This happens a lot with films. You can use a domestic distributor to manage rights in your country, but you may want to use various international distributors in regional markets where they are experts. Video and film projects can go even more granular, licensing rights to different media for the film, including streaming, digital downloads, television, educational, theatrical, non-theatrical, video on demand, retail, and home video. In some cases, such as streaming and digital downloads, you may have a non-exclusive deal with more than one distributor.

Splitting up the rights ensures that you can reach your audience in the variety of outlets they access creative works like yours. It gives you multiple revenue streams and distribution avenues for success, although each individual deal may be worth a bit less initially.

In some cases, splitting up rights may be easy. If you stream on a service like Twitch, for instance, you may want to save an archive to Twitch while also uploading that content to YouTube. That's sharing your video content on two services, and only requires a non-exclusive license. However, the more often you split up the rights, the more complicated deal-making can get. You should work with an attorney to ensure that the deals you're signing don't conflict with other deals you've already made. For example, if you already gave a distributor the exclusive rights in Chile for a specific time period, you can't give another party a license that conflicts with those rights, such as total worldwide rights during that time period. Splitting up rights can also be more work since you're having to do the work to make multiple distribution deals, rather than simply using an expert distributor who handles the entire deal making process.

That said, if you're concerned a single distributor might leave your work on the shelf, splitting up rights can ensure you maintain the flexibility to provide your content to your audience where and when they want it. In the digital age, attention is currency, and it's critical to be able to provide access to the creative work the moment someone is interested.

Self-distributing

Self-distribution is a more common choice than ever before, but it's hard work. Some creators simply want to cut out the middle man, and others want to make sure to reach their audiences in venues specifically relevant to the project. Did we mention it's hard work?

Self-distribution means you make the deals. If it's a film project, that means you're booking theatres, creating and selling merchandise, and making deals with broadcasters, streaming services, and others. If it's an e-book, you figure out the cover, layout, and illustrations. If it's a podcast, music, software, or a video game, you decide where to make it available, the pricing, and how to implement all the marketing that's needed to bring in audiences.

You get more of every dollar you make, but did we mention it's hard work? Self-distributing can be the equivalent of a full time job. The ease of distribution means that internet users are overwhelmed with information and creative content. Marketing and outreach then becomes a critical piece to getting your work seen, let alone making money.

Be honest with yourself. You may be an expert at your creative or business endeavor, but you may not be a marketing and distribution expert. That's ok. If you're self-distributing, consider consulting with experts in marketing and distribution to formulate a professional plan that gets you where you want to go.

No matter how you distribute, be thoughtful and careful with each deal. Make sure that the details you discussed by phone or email are reflected in the actual contract you sign. And if you're not sure if the legalese reflects that, be sure to get an attorney to help explain the agreement to you.

Part III
Crisis Mode

Chapter 15
You've Gotten a Nasty Lawyer Letter— Now What?

You've created your work, you thought you covered all of your bases, but then it happens. You open your inbox and there it is. It might just be an email or it might be a five page letter attached to an email but there's no mistaking it; it's a nasty lawyer letter. What do you do?!?!

While this chapter won't tell you exactly what to do in your particular situation (remember we didn't put any creepy privacy-invading, mind-reading into this book), it will break down many of the types of internet nastiness you may encounter and provide some basic dos and don'ts for responding.

The DMCA Takedown Notice

THE BOTTOM LINE

The Digital Millennium Copyright Act (DMCA) is a law that allows allegedly copyright infringing content to be removed from the internet simply by sending a letter to an internet service. While receiving a DMCA notice can be scary, there is an appeals process called a counternotice. But appealing can open you up to federal court litigation, so you should carefully consider appealing before you do.

As you may have read earlier in this book, the DMCA is a law that allows for, among other things, content to be taken down from the internet through a special process called notice and takedown. Depending on where your content is posted you'll either get an email from the platform it's posted on or an email directly from the copyright owner of the allegedly infringing work. This notice will usually let you know who sent it, their basic contact info, and what work was allegedly infringed.

Before you do anything, stop and take a breath!

Unless you have a secret time machine, it's impossible to go back and undo any knee-jerk reactions you may have, such as immediately appealing, slamming notice sender on social media, or burning all the copies of your content. For the record, burning things is rarely a good solution to any problem, legal or otherwise.

Check the claim for glaring errors.

Sometimes DMCA claims get made that are wildly inaccurate. Here are a few examples of red flags to watch out for:

1. **The copyright owner listed isn't a real person or company.**

   For example, DMCA claims from Darth Vader are less likely to be legitimate than claims from Lucas Films or Disney, the companies that hold the rights to Star Wars. However, keep in mind that copyright owners sometimes use third party companies like ZEFR or CDBaby, to enforce their rights. So the name you see may not always be the copyright owner.

2. **The copyrighted work claimed doesn't appear in your work.**

   For example, in 2003 the RIAA issued an apology after sending a strongly worded letter to Penn State University for distributing Usher songs.[34] In reality, the song in question was sung by an astronomy professor (also named Usher) about a Gamma ray satellite Professor Usher had helped to design, which sounds about as far from an Usher song as humanly possible.[35]

3. **You actually have a written license to use the work in question.**

   Sometimes copyright owners use automated services to perform takedowns. Some of these services are much better than others about asking copyright owners about existing licenses. If you receive a takedown for a work you have a license for you should reach out directly to your licensing contact for help resolving the issue.

---

34 Heins, Marjorie. "The Progress of Science and Useful Art: Why Copyright Today Threatens Intellectual Freedom." The Free Expression Policy Project, 2003. Web. 23 Feb. 2016. <http://www.fepproject.org/policyreports/copyright2d.pdf>.

35 Boyd, Padi, and Peter D. Usher. "Swift Song." AstroCappella. Web. 23 Feb. 2016. <http://www.astrocappella.com/swift.shtml>.

4. **It is your own content that was taken down by a company you hired to do your rights management.**

   While mistakes happen, it may be a sign to start looking for a new rights management company.

5. **It is your own content that was taken down by a random third party.**

   Sometimes internet trolls will file DMCA takedown notices to get works they don't like removed from the internet. Many service providers have caught onto this type of trolling and will not take down content after receiving this type of notice. However, some service providers do not evaluate takedowns so carefully, and may take the content down anyways.

   If your takedown has one of these glaring errors, you may want to consider appealing or, if appropriate, reaching out directly to the sender of the inaccurate notice.

If you did reuse a copyrighted work, was your reuse permitted?

Even if you don't have written permission to reuse the work; or aren't reusing a work under an open license like we discuss in Chapter 9, your reuse may still be allowed under certain limited circumstances.

1. **Public domain**

   As we discussed earlier, the public domain is a very limited category of works usually created before 1923. But just because it was from before 1923, doesn't necessarily mean it is in the public domain. For example, sound recordings weren't protected by copyright law until 1972 and no sound recordings will enter the public domain until 2067! If you're not sure if something is in the public domain, you may want to check out this awesome chart[36] or consult with an attorney.

2. **Fair use**

   As we discussed earlier, fair use allows for certain reuses of copyrighted works under specific circumstances. While online tools, like our very own Fair Use App[37], may be helpful, since fair use can be complex, and

---

36 "Copyright Term and the Public Domain in the United States." Cornell Copyright Information Center. Web. 23 Feb. 2016. <http://copyright.cornell.edu/resources/publicdomain.cfm>.

37 "The Fair Use App." New Media Rights, 15 July 2015. Web. 23 Feb. 2016. <http://newmediarights.org/fairuse/>.

someone is claiming copyright infringement, it's a good idea to reach out to an experienced copyright attorney for help assessing your fair use claim.

Should you counternotice or do something else?

If the claim is invalid for any of the reasons above, it may be time to appeal through a counternotice. But before you do, here are a few things to keep in mind:

1. **By counternoticing, you are swearing under penalty of perjury that law permits your reuse of the work**

   This means you are promising that you had a license, are reusing the work under fair use, or the work was in the public domain. If you're not 100% sure if your use was permitted, you may want to talk to a lawyer before appealing.

2. **By counternoticing you are agreeing that the other party can sue you in a federal court in the US**

   By filing a counternotice you are opening yourself up to a potential copyright lawsuit, so you need to be really sure that law permitted your reuse.

3. **By counternoticing you're starting a legal process**

   If the takedown is the result of a licensing dispute, it may be more efficient to reach out to your business contacts directly to discuss the issue.

If you did reuse a currently copyrighted work without permission outside the bounds of fair use, DO NOT COUNTERNOTICE! Some creators counternotice with the hope that their work will get put back up and nothing bad will happen. This is a lot like rocking a raw meat dress outside a bear cave at the end of hibernation season. There is a chance nothing bad will happen, but odds are there will be very painful consequences to your actions.

The Content ID takedown

Unlike the DMCA, which is law, ContentID is the specific internal system that YouTube uses for identifying copyrighted content. Many social media platforms now utilize some form of automated content identification like ContentID. When matching content is identified, it allows a copyright owner to mute, block or monetize the video. While it's getting better at content matching, it's no fair use wizard, and isn't always accurate or able to take fair use into account. Although the steps under the DMCA are largely relevant for assessing a Content ID situation, there are a few key differences to keep in mind.

1. **You're content won't necessarily get taken down.**

   Content can be muted or monetized. At the time of this writing, for songs that are monetized there is a process for splitting revenue between the copyright owner of the song being reused and the YouTube creator, but this has not been expanded to other types of content.

2. **Because ContentID is not law, the appeals process is regulated by YouTube.**

   There is no guarantee that an appeal will result in your content being restored.

3. **Appealing doesn't necessarily carry the same risk of litigation (because you do not have to consent to jurisdiction in a federal court).**

   Although, ContentID is intended as a tool to prevent copyright litigation against YouTube and its users, a copyright owner could still decide to file a lawsuit instead of using ContentID or after a successful ContentID user appeal.

Defamation

THE BOTTOM LINE

Your statement may be defamatory if it is a false factual statement. Keep in mind the bar for defamation is lower for private figures than public figures and you may want to seek out legal advice before responding to the claim.

Hopefully you read Chapter 12 on "Why you should care about being accurate and truthful" which included best practices for social media, and you took our tips to heart. But if you didn't (or even if you did) you might be accused of making a defamatory comment online. This section breaks down some of the steps you might want to take when you get that nastygram.

1. **As always, take a second to think before replying.**

   Your instinct may be to lash out or to profusely apologize, but doing either before you see if their claim has any merit could make solving the problem later more complicated.

2. **Make sure to keep records of all communications and have a copy of the content at issue.**

   It will be hard to get legal advice if you don't have this information because it makes it harder for an attorney to assess the issue.

3. **Get some good legal advice.**

   Defamation claims can be tricky and having an attorney help you evaluate them can often be the best way to go. They may be able to help you formulate a game plan for moving forward, even if you can only afford an initial consultation.

Trademark

THE BOTTOM LINE

Trademark law is all about protecting the consumer from confusion, but trademark claims made against you can be particularly confusing, so you may want to seek out legal advice before responding.

As we discussed earlier in this book, trademark law is all about protecting consumers from becoming confused, and purchasing the wrong product or service as a result of that confusion. Trademark disputes can be quite common on the internet and involve everything from URLs, advertising, art, and the sale of goods or services. So what should you do when you get a trademark nastygram?

1. **Take a moment to breathe!**

   We know we keep saying this, but not lashing out and instead replying with rational and coherent responses will help you to resolve the problem more quickly.

2. **But don't ignore the problem!**

   Many trademark letters contain deadlines for replying or taking action. While these deadlines may be arbitrarily set by the other party or their attorney, if you don't at least start the conversation with the other party before that deadline it will make resolving the situation amicably much harder.

3. **Make sure to keep records of the way you are allegedly using the trademark so you can seek out help from an attorney.**

4. **Seek out help from an attorney.**

   Trademark claims can be especially tricky. Even if you can't afford to retain an attorney, an initial consultation with one or more attorneys will at least help you get a better idea of whether you are infringing and how you should respond. Remember that trademark owners may be particularly over-aggressive in an effort to protect their trademark and keep it from becoming generic. Many trademark owners tend to go a bit overboard when doing this, pursuing any potential infringement large or small. This makes it particularly important to get legal advice before responding.

They're really angry... but I'm not sure why

THE BOTTOM LINE

Getting an incoherent angry email about your content or, even worse, a series of social media posts is never a pleasant experience but the worst thing in the world you can do is lash out at the sender without taking some time to evaluate their incoherent claims.

There you are minding your own business, when bam it hits your inbox; all caps, "creative" spelling and not so veiled accusations about your content. You think they're threats, but you are not exactly sure what they mean. While it may be tempting to just ignore it or fight back, these approaches could seriously hurt you if there is any validity to the claim. So what's a creator to do?

1. **Before you do anything stop and take a breath!**

   Replying while you're angry never leads to a good result in these types of cases.

2. **If your physical safety is at risk, call the police.**

   If the person made threats involving harm to your person or property, particularly if those threats include specifics details leading you to believe they may actually carry out those threats, go directly to the police department or your local FBI office for assistance.

3. **Take a moment to break down their claim.**

   Even if their argument is wrong, they may still have a legal claim. Think about whether this other person has any reason to be angry or is suggesting you violated the law. If either of those is true, or you're still not entirely sure, strongly consider reaching out to an attorneyfor advice.

4. **Make sure to keep records of all communications and have a copy of the content at issue.**

   It will be hard to get legal advice if you need it later on down the line if you don't have this information because it makes it harder for an attorney.

5. **If you do decide to reach out by email, be extremely polite.**

   While you shouldn't admit anything, it can sometimes be helpful to write an email to help clarify why they are upset and what they are requesting.

6. **Seriously, be polite!**

   In these types of disputes, it's not uncommon for parties (even those who have attorneys) to put your emails up on the internet as a way of pressuring you to do what they are asking.

7. **When in doubt, get legal advice.**

If you still don't know what's going on or if the other side is making demands you can't possibly comply with, consider hiring an attorney to help you resolve the situation.

You Just Got Served, Your First Lawsuit

THE BOTTOM LINE

Lawsuits, especially your first lawsuit, can be scary, time intensive, and expensive. That said, reacting calmly to address the situation can help resolve the situation more quickly.

1. **Don't panic!**

You may be noticing a trend here with our advice. Panicking tends to lead to people acting rashly and making bad decisions. If you need to, take a walk around the block or sleep on it and come back to things with fresh eyes.

2. **Don't ignore it!**

While ignoring problems rarely makes them go away, ignoring a lawsuit can be particularly problematic because a "default judgment" can be entered against you. What's a default judgment? A default judgment can occur when the person being sued does not respond in any way. At that point a judge can, and often does, decide the matter based on the documents the other party has prepared. This judgment can include anything from monetary damages against you, which could be handed over to a collection agency and affect your credit, to injunctions, which could result in the removal of your content or even prevent you from selling your product. So bottom line, you can't make things better if you don't show up.

3. **Don't start deleting, destroying, or fabricating potential evidence!**

There is sometimes a temptation to delete anything that could be incriminating, because what the other side can't know can't be used against you. This is, however, a very bad idea because destroying evidence after you have been sued is very, very illegal. For that matter, so is creating new, more flattering evidence to give the other party instead of the real evidence.

4. **Read the complaint.**

At least attempting to read the complaint may help you get a better idea of why you are being sued. There are also a few important things that you'll want to look for in the complaint.

- **Who is suing you?**
  Are you being sued by someone you don't recognize? You may need to sit down with your team to see if someone had contact with this other person or company.

- **Where are you being sued?**
  To help you find an attorney, it will be helpful to know both which state and city you are being sued in and what type of court you are being sued in. Most litigation-related attorneys are specialized to some extent, so your cousin who practices family law in Portland, Oregon's family law court won't be able to help you with a Copyright claim filed against you in a New York Federal Court.

- **Are there any deadlines listed?**
  Sometimes the document that the other party gives you may give you a deadline to reply by, but sometimes it won't. If a deadline is listed be sure to make a note of that date and be ready to reply. Don't panic if you don't understand everything in the complaint. There are attorneys and other resources that may be able to help you.

5. **Contact your insurance company.**

If you have insurance related to the dispute such as general business insurance or E&O insurance for a film, you'll want to make sure they are aware of the lawsuit. Some policies may deny coverage if the company is not notified in a timely manner of the lawsuit.

6. **Get a lawyer or at least preliminary legal advice.**

When it comes to litigation, it's best not to go it alone. Not only do success rates tend to be dismal for individuals who represent themselves with no legal advice or assistance, but if you are a company you may not be allowed to represent yourself depending on where you've been sued. But finding an attorney, especially when you don't know any, can be tricky. Here are some ideas to get you started in your search for an attorney.

- Ask friends and family for recommendations.

- Look on your state or county bar association website for details on their attorney referral programs.

- Certain specialized organizations offer referrals in cases of litigation. Some examples include The Electronic Frontier Foundation Attorney Referral Service[38] for legal matters related to the internet or technology and Volunteer Lawyers for the Arts[39], which is a loose network of nonprofits dedicated to helping artists with legal issues. Some legal aid programs also will provide referrals to attorneys with appropriate expertise.

- Some courts offer self-help offices staffed by attorneys who may be able to point you in the direction of attorneys or at the very least helpful resources. They may also be able to explain the legal documents that you have been served with.

This list is by no means an exhaustive list of options for finding an attorney, but we hope it serves as a helpful starting point in your search for legal representation to help you respond to the other parties' complaint.

What not to do when asking for legal help

If you get into trouble, you may need to reach out to an attorney. At NMR we field over 500 requests for legal services a year. While we're able to help many of those folks, we also see a few people who have misconceptions about the legal profession that make it much harder for them to get legal representation with us or otherwise. Some of these may seem obvious but they bear repeating to help you put your best foot forward when seeking legal representation.

---

38 "Legal Assistance from EFF." Electronic Frontier Foundation. Web. 23 Feb. 2016. <https://www.eff.org/pages/legal-assistance>.
39 "National VLA Directory." St. Louis Volunteer Lawyers and Accountants for the Arts. Web. 23 Feb. 2016. <http://vlaa.org/get-help/other-vlas/>.

1. **There are many types of lawyers; the first one you call may not be able to help.**

   Back in the day, many attorneys were generalists who worked in a wide variety of legal areas. Today, as laws evolve and become more specific, attorneys are more likely to specialize in certain areas. Even if an attorney comes highly recommended, if that attorney practices family law and you have a question about a YouTube takedown, you should probably find an attorney familiar with internet law and copyright law instead.

2. **Lawyers are very location specific if you live in Arizona, hiring the best contract lawyer in New York probably isn't helpful.**

   In the internet age, it can be shocking to many that attorneys in the US are regulated at the state level and not at the federal level. This means that in many cases you will need to hire an attorney licensed in your own state. There are some exceptions for certain types of federal law (like copyright or patent law) or litigation where attorneys may be able to provide limited services outside of states where they are licensed to practice.

3. **Tell the truth.**

   The truth may not be flattering, but your attorney will need to know it to help you in the most effective manner possible. By lying, you may make the situation worse and limit your options for efficiently solving your problem. Many attorneys will also simply end the representation if they find out the client lies to them.

4. **Don't ask an attorney to do something blatantly illegal for you.**

   While you shouldn't be asking anyone to do illegal things for you, you should never ask your attorney to do something illegal for you. In fact, if you do this in your initial consultation, many attorneys will stop the conversation there and ask you to leave their office.

5. **Don't threaten or yell at attorneys to get them to be your lawyer (Especially if you'd like free legal services).**

   Attorneys, especially pro bono and public interest attorneys, have finite resources. Cases get turned down for a variety of reasons, usually because the attorney doesn't have the resources or the expertise to take on the representation. Even if you're turned down by an attorney, many attorneys will still try to find a way to point you in the right direction.

Regardless, it's never useful to fire off an email full of profanities or threats after you've been turned down. You probably have a zero tolerance policy for harassment of your staff, and so do many law firms and legal non-profits. If you are rude to an attorney, or if you threaten an attorney, it is almost certain that attorney will not help you!

6. **Don't expect to get legal advice at a cocktail party or at a conference Q&A.**

   Whether it's over cocktails or in a ballroom at a conference, attorneys cannot give legal advice in a public setting due to confidentiality issues. It's completely ok to ask that attorney for their card and contact them later, but asking for legal advice in a public setting will just get you shut down in the politest way possible.

7. **Don't ask an attorney to sign an NDA before giving you legal advice.**

   In the startup world, NDAs are like cell phones: everybody has at least one. But unless you're hiring your attorney as in house counsel, you don't need to have your attorney sign an NDA because your attorney already owes you a duty of confidentiality. That means that attorney cannot share any information that you disclose to them outside of their law firm, except under very limited circumstances like preventing imminent physical harm to another person. Failing to keep a client's information confidential can lead to an attorney being disbarred (i.e. not allowed to be a lawyer anymore), which is a much scarier consequence for most attorneys than any penalty you can put in an NDA.

8. **Don't send an email blast to many attorneys at the same time.**

   Sometimes after getting a list of names from an attorney referral service a potential client will email everyone on the list in the same email lots of extremely confidential information about their case. Don't be that person! Many attorneys won't take these individuals on as clients because they made their confidential information widely available to a large number of people. This can cause problems later on and may even result in certain otherwise confidential information being turned over to the other side before trial.

9. **Be sure to keep all relevant documents and copies of content that you'd like advice about.**

Often we'll get approached about giving advice after content has been removed from the internet. Like many other attorneys, we have a hard rule against giving legal advice when we can't see the content. While this might seem unfair, an attorney can't give accurate legal advice when they don't understand the entire picture. In fact, receiving advice from an attorney who doesn't know all of the facts usually does more harm than good.

10. **Trust your attorney's judgment on the law, but give them all the facts.**

While attorneys love a well-informed, passionate client, if you're coming to an attorney it's usually because you have a question about the law. Telling an attorney all the reasons they are wrong in initial communications isn't conducive to getting that attorney to be your attorney. However, if the attorney makes a false assumption about the facts of your case (like if they say you have a written license when you actually just had oral permission), do let them know! Operating under bad assumptions isn't good for you or the attorney.

Again, while most of the tips above are common sense, we hope they help you from making some of the common mistakes people make when seeking legal representation.

Chapter 16
Responsible Enforcement: How to Handle Disputes Effectively Without Being a Troll

You think you've covered all your bases. You've got contracts in place, you registered your copyrights and trademarks, but then it happens. You may see your copyright or trademark reused without permission. You might be in a bind because, despite your carefully crafted contract, your videographer won't give you the video that you paid for. Or someone just might have said something really mean about you on the internet. What do you do?!?!

While this chapter won't tell you what to do in every situation, it will break down many of the types of disputes you may encounter and provide some basic suggestions for responding to those disputes.

General Tips

Before we get into some of the specific types of disputes you may encounter, here are some tips that apply across the board.

1. **Before you do anything, stop and take a breath!**

   We know, we know, we keep saying this but so many disputes become infinitely harder to solve because of unwise knee-jerk reactions.

2. **Don't contact the other party when you're angry.**

   Along those lines, though this may seem like common sense, belligerent emails, texts, tweets and snaps tend not to be the best way to solve any problems. Also keep in mind that certain bloggers really love to repost those belligerent communications, which could make solving your dispute harder. Take a beat or sleep on it before hitting send.

3. **Keep records of any materials related to the dispute.**

   Not only will this make it easier for you to get legal advice if you need it, but if the dispute goes to court later on intentionally destroying records could get you into trouble.

4. **Websites and apps aren't generally liable for illegal behavior by users.**

   Laws like the Digital Millennium Copyright Act Safe Harbor and the Communications Decency Act Section 230 protect websites and apps from a broad range of legal liability for illegal acts of their users. (for more info on these laws see Chapter 7) If you have a dispute with a user of a service, you may be able to get the service to take some action for you (say with a DMCA takedown notice or by using the service's flagging system). Outside of DMCA notices, which services are required to respond to, most actions that services take will be voluntary and not required by law. So be careful not to threaten legal consequences against a service without hiring an attorney who is experienced in internet law.

5. **When in doubt, seek out advice from an attorney.**

   Sometimes getting advice from an expert attorney, especially early in a dispute, can keep that dispute from escalating. It can even make the dispute quicker and easier to resolve.

Don't be Batman, and other helpful tips for responsibly enforcing your rights under copyright law online

Despite what you've seen on TV, showy speeches and nasty lawyer letters are often the worst way to resolve a copyright dispute. More often than not, creative ways of handling infringement when it arises are often better at combating copyright infringement.

Do

1. **Do make sure you are the copyright owner.**

   It may sound pretty basic but because only the copyright owner can enforce their copyright you'll want to make sure you actually own the copyright to your work.

2. **Make sure the work is actually infringing on your work.**

   Again, this may sound pretty basic but sometimes when your work is reused, it can be completely legal and non-infringing. Here are a few common enforcement mistakes:

- You've granted a license to someone to use your work and they are using according to the terms that license. This is not copyright infringement and you should not send a DMCA takedown notice (see Chapter 7).

- You've openly licensed your work and the person is reusing it under the terms of that open license. This is not copyright infringement and you should not send a DMCA takedown notice.

- Although the work has a similar sounding name, it is not, in fact, your work nor does it bear any relation to your work. This is not copyright infringement and you should not send a DMCA takedown notice.

- The reuse would likely be considered fair use. This is not copyright infringement and you should not send a DMCA takedown notice. If you're unsure whether the use is fair use you may want to reach out to an attorney for advice before you send that takedown notice.

3. **Think about turning an infringing use into a new business partnership.**

Not everyone who reuses your copyrighted work without permission is a dirty pirate out to steal your stuff. Often fans of a work will want to use your work just outside the bounds of fair use but may not know who to contact to get a proper license or even how to negotiate a license. Situations like this can be a great opportunity to consider entering into a new licensing agreement that you would have never entered into otherwise, keeping your fan base happy and your wallet healthy.

4. **Think about the business and PR ramifications.**

Not all infringements are created equal and nor do they merit the same response. For example, let's say a children's cancer ward had a local musician come in to do a "music time" event where he and the kids sang your songs without getting permission. Although this is technically copyright infringement, your reaction here should be very different than your reaction to someone pirating your music then posing as you to resell it on iTunes, for obvious reasons. Particularly where the use is non-commercial, used in a small setting or used by people who aren't legally savvy; even where there is copyright infringement there is often a more productive way to handle infringement. For instance, in the example above, offering to come in and do "music time" with the kids or donating a few CDs would have much better PR ramifications than sending a nasty letter to a kids cancer ward.

5. **Document the infringement and any communications with the other party.**

The moment you send a cease and desist letter or a DMCA takedown notice, there is a very high likelihood that the content will disappear. While this may be what you want, if you need to escalate things later it will be hard to do so unless you have some actual evidence of the infringement, so be sure to document the infringement before you send that notice. Similarly, you'll want to keep a record of any written correspondence you have with the other party just in case you need it later in court or to help your attorney better understand the situation.

6. **Register your copyright.**

Although you have to register your copyright before you bring a copyright lawsuit, there are two other reasons why promptly registering your copyright can help you enforce your rights under copyright law: attorneys' fees and statutory damages. If you register your work with the US copyright office prior to infringement or within 3 months of publication, these monetary awards could be available to you, which make it far easier to find an attorney to represent you.

- A special note about registration for bloggers, journalists, video creators, and others who create a lot of content: while registration is fairly cheap per work, in some cases as low as $35, if you create many works a month it can quickly get expensive to register everything. In this case you might register more selectively, including only the works you think will be most popular, or those that have already achieved popularity. An example might be a video creator whose channel has a few videos with hundreds of thousands of views consistently producing ad revenue, but many other videos that only have a few hundred total views. That video creator may choose to register just their most watched videos, as those are the videos that would be the most likely to be reproduced.

- If you need to file a lawsuit, get an attorney... But keep in mind there are other means of dispute resolution.

Because copyright law is exclusively federal law, the only place you can bring a copyright lawsuit is in federal court. The success rates for people who represent themselves in federal court are absolutely dismal. Your odds of success will be much higher with a skilled copyright attorney on your side. That said, other forms of dispute resolution, such as mediation, could often be better, less expensive and more effective choices where none of the parties involved have the resources to litigate the matter in court.

Don't

1. **Don't be Batman!**

   There is a saying on the internet that you should always be yourself unless you can be batman, then you should be batman. When it comes to copyright infringement, sometimes people who aren't the copyright owner want to put on their superhero capes and fight for the rights of copyright owners whose rights were infringed without the knowledge of the copyright owner. This is a bad idea. Only the copyright owner is allowed to enforce their copyrights, not even the coolest of spandex clad vigilantes can enforce another person's copyrights without their knowledge. You may feel the need to let the copyright owner know, but please don't be Batman.

2. **Don't take drastic measures just because you think you'll lose your copyright.**

   You have no risk of losing your copyright for failing to enforce your rights. Often a more measured polite email is a better way to resolve solutions then going in guns blazing.

3. **Don't send a takedown because you don't agree with what was said.**

   The right to prevent other people from saying mean things about your work is not one of the rights granted by copyright laws, nor is it a valid reason to send a DMCA takedown notice.

4. **Don't send a takedown notice as a way of resolving a licensing dispute.**

   Even the most well written license can still result in a dispute. There are many ways of resolving licensing disputes, including talking to the other party and renegotiating the license. If you read Chapter 8 about

"How to License Anything", hopefully you have a clear, human-readable agreement you can revisit to resolve your dispute. Although you may need to send a takedown if all other efforts fail, sending a takedown should not be your first move.

5. **Don't be afraid to stand your ground against a larger entity if they infringed your work.**

   Sometimes large content owners, even those who pour millions into squelching every reuse of their work, legal or illegal, reuse the works of creators without permission. This is particularly common with things like viral videos. Although it may seem hopeless, if that larger entity infringed your copyright don't be afraid to stand up for your rights. They should at least be willing to play by their own rules.

6. **Be careful when hiring a company to enforce your rights online.**

   There are many small companies purporting to help copyright owners crawl the internet to find, monetize and/or takedown infringing content. Not all of these companies are created equal. If you decide to use one of these services, do your research and particularly try to avoid companies who have a record of accidently taking down the creators' own works or properly licensed works. Also be sure to ask if they have any method for screening for probable fair uses so you avoid the PR disasters we talked about above.

Although not exhaustive, we hope this list of do's and don'ts proves helpful if you find yourself in the unpleasant position of having to enforce your copyrights.

Just because it's mean doesn't mean it's illegal, and other helpful tips for responsibly responding to defamation online.

No one likes it when people say mean things about them, especially on the internet. But being mean isn't always illegal and it often does not amount to defamation. Here are some things to think about before pursuing a defamation claim.

7. **Do make sure the statement is a provable fact.**

   While having someone say something mean about you on the internet is never fun, if the crux of their statement is not a provable fact, however mean their statement is, IT IS NOT DEFAMATORY. For example, it may hurt your feelings if someone called you a Grumpy Pants McGee, but because it is not a provable statement of fact it is not defamatory.

8. **Don't pursue a claim if that fact was truthfully stated.**

   The truth hurts, but pursuing a defamation claim when someone published the truth will hurt you even more.

9. **Don't use the DMCA or non-defamation tools to resolve a defamation related dispute.**

   At best this will confuse your attacker, and at worst they could bring any number of claims against you for making false claims.

10. **Do get an attorney if you need one, but be open to resolving the dispute outside of a courtroom.**

    Although defamation claims can be resolved in state court and a litigator may be able to help you with that, a good attorney will talk you through different and potentially less expensive ways of resolving your dispute, like mediation.

11. **Be prepared for the entire dispute to show up on the internet.**

    Although not fun for the parties involved, defamation cases tend to make pretty great news stories due to the salacious mudslinging. Handling the dispute poorly or over aggressively increases these odds and can draw more attention to the statement you wanted to make disappear in the first place.

Although not exhaustive, we hope this list of tips proves helpful if you find yourself in the unpleasant position of having people say horrible, defamatory things about you.

Yes they can use your trademark to talk about your product, and other helpful tips for responsibly enforcing your trademark rights online.

Trademarks can be expensive to get, more expensive to protect, and disastrous to your business if you lose protection. Because of these factors trademark over enforcement has become a bit of an epidemic, but it doesn't have to be that way! Here are some tips for enforcing your trademarks responsibly online.

1. **Make sure they're actually infringing on your trademark.**

   Again, this may sound pretty basic but sometimes when your trademark is reused, it can be completely legal and non-infringing. Here are a few common enforcement mistakes:

   - **You've granted a license to someone to use your trademark and they are using it according to the terms of that license.** This is not trademark infringement, and you should not send that person a nasty letter.

   - **Although the work, product, or service has a similar sounding name, it is not, in fact, using your trademark; it does not bear any relation to your trademark nor is any consumer likely to be confused by the use.** For example, let's say you have a trademark on your San Diego, California ramen shop name "Hipster Owl's Ramen Shop," and someone else has a band called "The Hipster Owls Take Brooklyn by Unicycle." Although both trademarks are painfully hipster, it is highly unlikely that anyone would confuse a band with a ramen shop.

   - **Your trademark doesn't appear anywhere, you just don't like what is being said.** This is not a trademark issue at all and should not be treated like one.

   - **The reuse is otherwise permissible under trademark law.** Many times if the reuse is directly and accurately referring to your product or service, not simply using your mark or a portion of your mark to sell a competing product or service, it isn't infringement (this is known as "nominative" use). Also, if someone else simply uses a word in your mark in its normal sense that's not infringement either. So if an organic fruit stand puts out a sign that says "Buy apples here!" that is not an infringement of the Apple Corporation's trademarks (this is known as descriptive trademark fair use). If you're unsure whether the use is permissible you may want to reach out to an attorney for advice before acting.

2. **Think about turning an infringing use into a new business partnership.**

   Not everyone who reuses your trademark without permission is a counterfeiter. Often fans of a work will want to use your work just outside the bounds of permissible uses but may not know who to contact to get a proper license or even how to negotiate a license.

Situations like this can be a great opportunity to consider entering into a new licensing agreement that you would have never entered into otherwise; keeping your fan base happy and your wallet healthy.

1. **Think about the business and PR ramifications.**

   Not all infringements are created equal and nor do they merit the same response. Sometimes sending a polite email or even making a simple call will help resolve the situation faster than having your lawyer write the scariest letter they can.

2. **Document the infringement and any communications with the other party.**

   The moment you send a cease and desist letter, there is a very high likelihood that the problematic use of your trademark will disappear. While this may be what you want, if you need to escalate things later it will be hard to do so unless you have some actual evidence of the infringement, so be sure to document the infringement before you send anything. Similarly, you'll want to keep a record of any written correspondence you have with the other party just in case you need it later in court or to help your attorney better understand the situation.

3. **Be careful when hiring a company to enforce your rights online.**

   There are many small companies purporting to help trademark owners crawl the internet to find, monetize and/or takedown infringing content. Not all of these companies are created equal. If you decide to use one of these services do your research and particularly try to avoid companies who have a record of accidently taking down their clients' websites, products or properly licensed works. Also be sure to ask if they have any method for screening for probable permissible uses so you avoid the PR disasters we talked about above.

4. **Don't take drastic measures just because you think you'll lose your trademark.**

   Although as a trademark owner you do have to defend your trademark to keep it, there is a big difference between enforcing your trademark so it doesn't become generic and trying to squash every potential use of your trademark. For example, you probably shouldn't treat a notorious international counterfeiter the same way you would a fan who released a free knitting pattern containing one of your trademarks.

5. **Don't send a cease and desist letter because you don't agree with what was said about your trademark.**

   The right to prevent other people from saying mean things about your good or service is not one of the rights granted by trademark law.

6. **If you need to file a lawsuit, get an attorney…But keep in mind there are other means of dispute resolution.**

   Trademark lawsuits are particularly complicated so if you need to file a trademark lawsuit you should hire and experienced trademark litigator. That said, other forms of dispute resolution, such as mediation, can often be better, less expensive and more effective choices where none of the parties involved have the resources to litigate the matter in court.

Although not exhaustive, we hope this list of tips proves helpful if you find yourself in the unpleasant position of having to enforce your trademark.

A word about contract disputes.

Even if you've taken the time to draft a clear, concise and fair contract; a dispute may still arise. On the bright side, if you have a contract it should be much easier to resolve the dispute because the contract should have a dispute resolution clause to give you a map for how the dispute should be resolved. But not everyone is good at following directions. If the other party to the contract isn't working with you to resolve the problem according to the contract; you may need to get an attorney. Sometimes, if the contract is for a small amount of money and the other party's breach of the terms is clear, you may consider pursuing such a dispute in small claims court.

A word about lawsuits.

Unfortunately, even if you take a responsible and measured approach to enforcement, you still may need to go to court and sue someone. Litigation can be ugly, uncertain, long, and complicated so you'll want to make sure you have an attorney to represent you, and consider all other possible options before filing that lawsuit.

Enforcing your rights is never a fun process, but hopefully this chapter has provided you with some helpful tips for enforcing your rights responsibly.

Conclusion

Congrats! You made it to the end of the book! You now know some of the major legal stumbling blocks you may run into over the course of your creative or entrepreneurial venture and most importantly, you know when you might need to call a lawyer for help. Before you go, we wanted to take just a moment to remind you that New Media Rights is a small independently funded non-profit operating on a shoestring budget and we rely on individual donors to support our work. Donations from individuals like you help us provide critical legal services to creators who may otherwise go without. By purchasing this book you've already helped New Media Rights but if you've enjoyed this book and want to make sure New Media Rights legal services are available to the creators and entrepreneurs who would otherwise go without, consider becoming a New Media Rights Supporter today![40]

If a donation isn't financially feasible at the moment, there are still other ways you can help! Please take a moment and tell others about us on Twitter[41], Facebook[42], YouTube[43] and other social media sites. Often people don't know where to turn when they run into legal issues and your kind words about us on social media (or in real life) can help connect us with some of the people that need us the most!

---

40 "Support Levels & Benefits." New Media Rights, 1 Feb. 2016. Web. 23 Feb. 2016. <http://newmediarights.org/support_levels_benefits>.

41 "New Media Rights Twitter." *Twitter*. New Media Rights. Web. <https://twitter.com/newmediarights>.

42 "New Media Rights Facebook." *Facebook*. New Media Rights. Web. <http://facebook.com/newmediarights>.

43 "New Media Rights YouTube." *YouTube*. New Media Rights. Web. <https://www.youtube.com/user/newmediarightsstudio>.

Acknowledgments

We'd like to take a moment to acknowledge just a few of the people who helped make this book a success. First we'd like to acknowledge our student interns and former staff who helped us write and research this book, including the many interns whose work served as inspiration for this book. We'd like to especially acknowledge Erika Lee, Cara Laursen, Emory Roane, Joelle Bartkins, Leopoldo Gabriel Estrada, and Nicholas J. Petruolo, who each assisted significantly with this book. Special thanks also go to Shaun Spalding whose work at New Media Rights informed this book, as well as Cy Kuckenbaker and Alexander Johnson for their invaluable feedback. We'd also like to thank California Western School of Law for being an amazing home and partner for the New Media Rights program.

Finally, Art would like to specifically thank his wife Arianna, whose partnership made New Media Rights and this book possible. Art also thanks his son, parents, sister, New Media Rights Advisory Board, and friends for their support. Teri would like to thank her fiancé, parents, brother and friends for their constant support, particularly putting up with her during her hustle to get this book out the door.

About the Illustrator

Batton Lash

Batton Lash is the creator of the humor/horror series Supernatural Law (aka Wolff & Byrd, Counselors of the Macabre). Lash has also written for Archie Comics and comic books featuring The Simpsons and The Pink Panther. His latest creator-owned property is The First Gentleman of the Apocalypse, a brand-new series Lash created for David Lloyd's online comics anthology Aces Weekly. More on Batton Lash can be found at www.exhibitapress.com

About the Authors

Art Neill

Art is the founder of New Media Rights, and practices public interest law in the areas of internet, intellectual property, privacy, and media law. Art is also an adjunct professor of law at California Western School of Law teaching the courses Internet & Social Media Law as well as the Internet & Media Law Clinic.

In 2011, 2013, and 2015 Art was appointed as a member of the Federal Communication Commission's Consumer Advisory Committee, where he has served as Co-chair of the Broadband Working Group. In 2014, Art was named to the Fastcase 50, which honors the law's smartest, most courageous innovators, techies, visionaries, & leaders. Art received his J.D. from University of San Diego School of Law in 2006, and his B.A. from the College of William & Mary in 2001. Click here[44] to learn more about Art, including publications, interviews, honors, and presentations. You can also check out his LinkedIn profile here[45] and his SSRN page here[46].

---

44 "Art Neill. New Media Rights, 27 Feb. 2016. Web. 23 Feb. 2016. <http://www.newmediarights.org/about_us/nmr_staff/art_neill>.
45 "Art Neill." New Media Rights, 10 Mar. 2016. Web. 10 Mar. 2016 <https://www.linkedin.com/in/art-neill-3203b57>
46 "Author Page for Art Neill." Social Science Research Network, 10 Mar. 2016. Web. 10 Mar. 2016. <http://ssrn.com/author=1346806>

Teri Karobonik

Teri is a Staff Attorney at New Media Rights where she works with all manner of creative individuals on a daily basis on preventative, transactional and pre-litigation matters. In addition to one-on-one assistance Teri actively engages in policy work with the copyright office as well as educational work. Teri is also an adjunct professor of law at California Western School of Law where she co-teaches the Internet & Media Law Clinic. In 2015 Teri was appointed as an Internet Law & Policy Foundry Fellow in recognition of her work as an early career leader in the tech law and policy space.

Teri received her J.D. from Santa Clara Law in 2012. While she was at Santa Clara Teri earned numerous awards for her work in IP and Privacy including a Pro-Bono Award for her work as the International Legal Intern at the Electronic Frontier Foundation in the summer of 2011. Teri received her B.A. with honors in Creative Writing from the University of Arizona in 2009. She was also inducted into Phi Beta Kappa. For more on Teri click here[47] for her full bio you can also check out her LinkedIn profile here[48] and her SSRN page here[49].

47 "Teri Karobonik." New Media Rights, 27 Feb. 2016. Web. 23 Feb. 2016. <http://newmediarights.org/teri_karobonik>.
48 "Teri Karobonik." LinkedIn, 23 Feb. 2016. Web. 23 Feb. 2016. <http://www.linkedin.com/pub/teri-karobonik/13/881/55a>.
49 "Author Page for Teri Karobonik." Social Science Research Network, 23 Feb. 2016. Web. 23 Feb. 2016. <http://goo.gl/KMfdMw>.

Made in the USA
Charleston, SC
28 December 2016